MIRACLES OF THE AMERICAN REVOLUTION

DIVINE INTERVENTION AND THE BIRTH OF THE REPUBLIC

LARKIN SPIVEY

GOD & COUNTRY
PRESS

An Imprint of
AMG Publishers

Miracles of the American Revolution: Divine Intervention and the Birth of the Republic

Published by God and Country Press (an imprint of AMG Publishers)
6815 Shallowford Road
Chattanooga, Tennessee 37421

Published in association with the literary agency of Credo Communications, LLC. (www.credocommunications.net).

First printing, June 2010
ISBN 13: 978-0-89957-021-1

Maps by Bowring Cartographic, 258 North Park Dr., Arlington, VA 22203. www.sitemaps.com
Cover design by Michael Largent, Indoor Graphics Corp.,
Interior design and typesetting by Reider Publishing Services, West Hollywood, California.

Edited and proofread by Sharon Neal and Rick Steele.

Printed in Canada
16 15 14 13 12 11 10 –T– 7 6 5 4 3 2 1

DEDICATION

This book is dedicated to the *Miracles* in my life:

To my forevermore love, friend, partner, and wife: Lani.

To the greatest children that a man could be blessed to have: Windom, Catherine Alexa, Bayliss, and Anastasia.

To family members that I treasure: Ken, Lara, Daniel, Stephanie, Sophie, Owen, Charlotte, Annabelle, Larkin, Radik, Calder, Cousteau, and babies Rountree and Spivey.

Thanks to every one of you for making my life worthwhile and for always inspiring me with your unique gifts and strength of character. I love you and pray that God will grant to each of you in your own life, "an humble heart, a steadfast purpose, and a joyful hope."

TABLE OF CONTENTS

LIST OF MAPS

PREFACE

THE MESSAGE of this book is simple: Divine intervention has influenced America's history. To some this may be a dubious assertion and to others, a blinding glimpse of the obvious. In writing this book I have tried to keep the former, more skeptical, attitude at the forefront of my thoughts. I can assure readers with this viewpoint that the historical information presented, even though often astounding, is always factual.

I previously wrote *God in the Trenches* to give evidence of God's hand in America's history during the Revolutionary War, Civil War, World War II, and the Cold War. These episodes were at turning points in those wars and were crucial to America's survival. This book returns to the beginning and most crucial period of all: the American Revolution. During the period of its founding, an incredible collection of men and events shaped the destiny of America. I believe that words such as *random* or *fortunate* are wholly inadequate to describe this phenomenon. All would agree that America is a great nation. We should also wonder why.

God in the Trenches was published in 2001 shortly after the crisis of September 11. Since then, America has engaged in ongoing armed conflict. During this period, I have seen media and public interest that reflects an emergent curiosity about the subject of God and war. I hear the question repeatedly: Is God on America's side today? I will offer my answer to this question later, but the pervasiveness of the question itself reflects an urgency to understand more about God and his relationship to this nation.

Possibly this sense of urgency is stimulated by the specter of Muslim terrorists willing to die for their own religious beliefs. Today, Americans find such extremism difficult to comprehend. Americans do not consider the war on terrorism to be a religious war, and they do not consider Muslims to be enemies. Still, there is an undeniable interest in the religious aspects of our present conflict. We know that we have enemies willing to die for jihad, or holy war. Is there anything this important to Americans? Does America stand for anything in the moral or religious sense? This book will suggest answers to these questions, but, more importantly, will seek to stimulate interest in the questions themselves.

My foremost purpose in writing this book is to tell the remarkable story of America's founding and to illuminate the source of America's greatness. I stand in company with most of the founding fathers themselves in believing that Divine Providence was at the center of this seminal historical event.

I pray that God looks favorably on this effort and that someday he will reveal the complete story of his intervention in human history.

A NOTE FOR SKEPTICS

(Like the one you get with your junk mail: "Read this before
you decide *not* to accept the enclosed offer!")

A S MENTIONED in the preface, I am very conscious
that you probably find the premise of this book doubt-
ful, at best. As a skeptical person for most of my life,
my attitude has been the same. Show me the facts. Let me make
my own conclusions. I want to assure you again that this book
is written in that spirit. My primary focus is on actual historical
information. I do draw conclusions, but I also encourage you to
formulate your own. There is no assumption that you have the
same beliefs as I have.

If you are a true skeptic, you have an open mind and are
constantly seeking new knowledge. I hope that your search at
least allows for the possibility of spiritual truth. There are certain
questions that cannot be answered through intellectual effort
alone. Scientists may someday figure out how the universe came
to exist. However, they will never discover why.

If you wonder how a skeptical person ever taps into this
spiritual world, I can offer the key provided by the master. Jesus
said that, "Unless you come as a child, you will never enter the
kingdom of heaven." He is not suggesting that you put aside
your intellect. Far from it. He is suggesting that you study the

world around you with an appropriate sense of wonder. Any facet of the natural world, when considered deeply, is magnificently complex and ordered. A child might say *miraculous.*

I hope that you will continue reading to learn about the magnificently complex men and events that contributed to the founding of America, and why I might consider them miraculous. I invite you to ponder my interpretations and to think further about your own. At the very least I promise you will be uplifted by an incredible story.

—L.S.

PART ONE
THE IDEAS

CHAPTER ONE
CALL TO FREEDOM

"The sacred rights of mankind are not to be rummaged for among old parchments or musty records. They are written, as with a sunbeam, in the whole volume of human nature, by the hand of divinity itself, and can never be erased or obscured by mortal power."

—ALEXANDER HAMILTON[1]

"Kings and Parliaments cannot give the rights essential to our happiness. We claim them from a higher source—from the King of kings, and Lord of all the earth. They are created in us by the decrees of Providence, which establish the laws of our nature."

—JOHN DICKINSON[2]

THE BEGINNING

In 1763 the British Empire emerged victoriously from the Seven Years' War as the dominant power in the world. The Treaty of Paris confirmed British control over India and most of North America, including Canada, Florida, and the vast territory lying west of the American colonies to the Mississippi River. Standing behind this expanded worldwide trading empire was a great army and the most powerful navy in the world.

Political strength was also a vital ingredient of British power, resulting from continued advancements toward representative government. More active Parliaments and an evolving constitution had constrained the powers of the monarchy. A dynamic competition was ongoing between the interests of the Crown, the landed aristocracy, the church, and the successful merchants and traders.

In 1763 most colonists in America were content, and even proud, to be Englishmen and loyal subjects to royal authority. There was widespread appreciation for Britain's protection of the western territories and for elimination of the French threat. There were common bonds of culture, language, and religion, and a shared birthright of protection under English law. The estimated population of England was then six million, and the colonies about half that.[3] However, the New World with its vast expanse of new territory represented the growth potential of the future. The future looked bright for the North American colonies as the most dynamic component of a British Empire in its ascendancy.

Within two decades this picture changed drastically as the result of one of the most remarkable reverses in history. Within this brief span, disaffection grew among the Americans to the point of armed revolt and war. An alliance was formed with France, the historic enemy of both the colonies and England. The colonies renounced their allegiance to the English king and church, as well as all the benefits of English citizenship. In 1763 very few on either side of the Atlantic could have anticipated this reversal.

What could have driven the Americans to such a break? How could a group of culturally and economically disparate colonies come together to confront and prevail over the foremost military establishment in the world? How could an all-powerful

Great Britain lose control of her most vital territory and all that it promised for the future? These are questions that have consumed historians over the centuries. Historians have sought and continue to seek their answers in the complex attitudes and events of the time and in the interplay of economic, cultural, philosophical, and military developments. There are volumes and even libraries devoted to these subjects.

GOD'S PERSPECTIVE

The purpose of this book is to seek to understand God's influence over the great men and events of the American Revolution. I do not presume this to be a simple undertaking. These were complex men and complicated events, and different interpretations are possible. The fervent believer may see God's hand in all things. The religious skeptic, on the other hand, sees a natural reason for everything. The truth is not as simple as either view. I believe that God does control history, but that he does not usually manipulate human behavior or events openly or directly.

In accordance with his own purpose, God created human beings with the capacity of mind to make choices and decisions. With this freedom of will, humanity has achieved much that is good. Unfortunately, this freedom also allows human actions that are thoughtless, misguided, and even evil. I believe that most of what we see routinely happening in the world is the product of either human actions or natural forces.

So, how do we know when God intervenes in the affairs of the world? It is obviously not always easy to discern. My viewpoint comes from the experience of his influence in my own life and also from what I have seen in the lives of others. I usually perceive his presence when I seek it through prayer. His answers come in his time and in his way. His influence is usually subtle and best discerned through introspection. Often I see his hand in retrospect when examining past events, just as I more clearly see changes in myself and in my own life when looking back. I believe that the same approach can reveal God's hand in shaping the broader tapestry of history.

God works through history in accordance with his own plan and his own agenda. We never understand completely what that plan is, particularly at the time of its unfolding. Historians have the advantage of being able to look back in time to see the outcome of events. With the perspective offered by time we have the opportunity to discern patterns shaping those events. Careful examination of the history of the North American colonies before and during the American Revolution reveals many such amazing patterns.

GOD'S AGENDA

Since the creation, God's agenda for humanity has been freedom. By his own design he made human beings with the mental capacity to wonder about the heavens and infinity and even God himself. The human mind is also capable of making choices and decisions in everyday life. In biblical terms, God made us in his own image, and our highest purpose is to experience God through a relationship with him.

Freedom is integral to this design. If God had wanted robots he would have programmed humans to act only on his command. If he wanted to control our relationship with him he would appear regularly to issue instructions. He does neither. Apparently, God considers the concept of a person's relationship to him, or faith in him, meaningless without the freedom to choose. Freedom means responsibility and uncertainty. It gives the capacity to act in accordance with God's purpose or against it. By providing this capacity, God unfortunately made the human condition difficult.

Throughout history, and particularly the history of Western civilization, governments and religious institutions have routinely ignored this fundamental aspect of human nature in the establishment of authority in the world. Civil and religious liberty have been rare conditions. The thrust instead has been toward the concentration of power, usually for the sake of order and collective security. Power has also been important in the religious sphere as leaders have been driven to maintain conformity, or in their eyes purity, of belief and practice. This religious authority was wielded exclusively by the Catholic Church for centuries until the Reformation. Then many Protestant churches exercised the same authority as soon as they were able.

In Europe before the eighteenth century the power of church and state were usually combined, each supporting the other at the national level. European monarchs consolidated their kingdoms under the banner of the church and its divine blessing. Church leaders enhanced their own standing and that of the church through these alliances. The freedom of the individual to personally find God was not the agenda of many or even most church or civic leaders. Even so, it continued to be God's agenda.

FREEDOM IN AMERICA

Settlers came to the new world in search of new lives and new opportunities. Usually they were subject to some form of royal authority, which they rarely questioned. Church authority was another matter. Many of the American colonies were founded specifically as a refuge for those unable to live and grow spiritually under the conditions existing in Europe. Calvinist separatists, or "pilgrims," came to Plymouth via Holland in 1620 motivated to find a place where they could worship freely. Waves of "puritans" fleeing official repression in England came during the 1630s and 40s. The second Lord Baltimore established Maryland in 1634 with specific guarantees of religious toleration, first attracting Catholics and then various other Christian groups. William Penn founded Pennsylvania in 1681 as a "holy experiment" and a haven for all forms of religion, attracting large numbers of Quakers and other minority Christian groups from many European countries. French Protestants, or Huguenots, came in large numbers to Massachusetts, New York, and South Carolina after Catholic dominance was reasserted in France in 1685.[4]

All who came were not dissidents, however. The religious establishment also came to the New World. Anglicans came to bring the Church of England first to Virginia and then to the other colonies. In the early 1700s the Society for the Propagation of the Gospel was supporting over three hundred Anglican missionaries spread from Georgia to New England.[5] Many of these missionaries went into communities where other churches already existed. This created a lot of ill will among churchgoers who thought their own congregations were being proselytized. In spite of resistance, the effort continued to spread the official church throughout the colonies.

Another phenomenon developed to curtail some of the spiritual freedom of the early colonies. As the churches became more settled and organized, many began to evidence their own intolerance toward dissent. Particularly in New England, there was little patience with those not conforming to established religious practice. The mainstream churchgoers felt that dissenters could practice their beliefs elsewhere. Heresy trials were held frequently, and banishment was common practice.[6]

Due to separation from England and the existence of a wide variety of churches, the religious establishment in the colonies was not as uniform as that in the Old World. However, the tendency to mingle church and civic power remained strong. Religious ties to governmental authority not only continued, but seemed to increase in many areas with time.

The American Revolution brought the overthrow of European political and religious establishments in America. The political issues are well known and will be referred to often in later chapters. However, I believe that the religious issues were the most important part of God's agenda. One purpose of this book is to show how the complex process leading to religious freedom was central to the Revolution and fundamental to the future of America.

In the 1700s powerful conflicting forces came together to finally set the direction of religion in America. The Great Awakening worked within the body of the church community itself to increase spirituality and to loosen the ties of establishment.[7] The Enlightenment came from outside the church and directly challenged spirituality.

THE GREAT AWAKENING

An amazing wave of spiritual revival swept the American colonies during the 1730s and '40s. This phenomenon began as a series of widely separate episodes of Christian renewal. Within the Dutch Reformed Church in New Jersey Frederick Theodore Freylinghuysen preached a message of individual salvation transcending church orthodoxy. Gilbert Tennant brought a spiritual message to the Presbyterian Church emphasizing that there was more to pleasing God than the formalities of church membership. In New England Jonathan Edwards led a revival with similar themes.

All of these separate movements took a larger focus when George Whitefield came to America from England in 1738.[8] Whitefield was an Anglican and an unforgettable preacher who felt the call to take his message outside the formal church into public and open-air settings. On his mission he journeyed across the Atlantic thirteen times preaching his message of personal salvation up and down the East Coast.

The efforts of Whitefield and these other evangelists inspired itinerant preachers to travel throughout the colonies preaching that true religion was in individual repentance and a personal relationship with God. The message was clear that God does not work through kings, bishops, and clergymen, but among the people themselves. The message fell on receptive ears as crowds flocked to these preachers.[9]

These itinerant preachers of the Awakening carried no sanction of church authority. They had only the spiritual authority of the Bible and their own persuasiveness. They recognized that no act of repentance was meaningful without the complete free will of the individual. The Awakening seemed to draw large numbers of people throughout the colonies back toward a more direct relationship to God based on their willing and personal acceptance of his forgiveness.[10]

The Great Awakening brought new ideas and energy to the colonial churches and sparked new resistance to the established congregations. More citizens felt increased dissatisfaction with the idea of toleration of minority religious groups and taxation in support of the official churches. These attitudes had a distinct bearing on the revolution to come.

This revival phenomenon also had a direct link to the Revolution through the College of New Jersey at Princeton. The Presbyterian Church established this institution in 1746 as a direct outgrowth of the Great Awakening. James Madison studied there under its famous headmaster, John Witherspoon, both subjects of chapter two. Through these men religious freedom became one of the prime motives and foundational aspects of the Revolution.

THE ENLIGHTENMENT

A group of seventeenth- and eighteenth-century European philosophers and scientists were associated with a philosophical movement now referred to as the Enlightenment. Historians also call this period the Age of Reason. There was a belief shared by these men that the world was emerging from centuries of darkness into a new age in which human reason and science would solve all mankind's problems. Sir Isaac Newton epitomized this movement as he solved the great questions of astronomy, physics, and mathematics. The French philosophers, including Montesquieu and Voltaire, were particularly dominant figures of the Enlightenment.

Inherent to Enlightenment thought was an antipathy toward anything that restricted scientific and philosophical inquiry. The persecutions of Galileo, Newton, and Descartes for scientific opinions that tended to undermine religious orthodoxy were well known at the time. Church dogma and religious establishments that demanded conformity of thought and practice came under scrutiny and attack.

The concept of faith and revelation in religion also came under attack. Any belief that could not pass the test of reason was not considered valid. Most of revealed religion failed this test. Still, some Enlightenment thinkers considered God a reasonable concept if viewed as the "master watchmaker." This was the force that designed the universe and set it in motion, but did not then continue to make adjustments to it or to interfere with mankind and nature.[11]

Chapter two will show that practically every revolutionary founder was well versed in these Enlightenment ideas. All seemed to respond to the emphasis on reason and the importance of free inquiry in science and religion. However, most had no difficulty incorporating reason and religious faith into their own lives. Only Jefferson seemed to lean toward a pure deism with a complete disavowal of a personal God.

These crosscurrents of spiritual awakening and philosophical questioning that came together in America during the 1700s are apparently contradictory. One led to a deeper spirituality. One undermined spirituality. However, these currents were brought together and integrated into a marvelous pattern to accomplish a great purpose. Chapter two will explain how these currents combined to establish the foundation of America's freedom: the sacred free choice of the individual conscience before God.

OVERVIEW

History often seems inevitable in retrospect. We know who won the Revolutionary War, and it is difficult to imagine any other result. The British were defeated and the United States of America was founded. How could it have been otherwise? We dispel the apparent inevitability of this great historic event when we carefully examine the details.

History is not unique in this respect. Any subject has its superficial aspect until explored in depth. Most of us give little thought to our own bodies. However, years of study reveal a wondrous intricacy to the doctor. In like manner, the natural world opens up to the biologist and the stars to the astronomer. The details of history also reveal an awesome complexity and show the precarious nature of many great events.

The purpose of this book is to show the complex pattern of men and events integral to the founding of America. It is an astounding and miraculous pattern. The end result was a new nation based on a new order of freedom unseen before in the world. The odds against this outcome were immense. Part two is about the men and ideas that somehow came together at the right time and place. Part three is about the military struggle. Each clash was crucial, and each reveals more about the precarious nature of America's march to freedom and the presence of God's providential hand at each critical moment. Part four summarizes the miracles of the Revolution and considers the implications of this history to America's current condition and future direction.

PART TWO
THE MEN

CHAPTER TWO

FOUNDERS

"The contest with Britain begot in the course of a dozen years the most remarkable generation of public men in the history of the United States or perhaps of any other nation . . . an explanation of the phenomenon lies beyond the wit of the historian."

—ARTHUR SCHLESINGER[12]

HISTORIANS LOOK in wonder at the men who presided over the American Revolution. One expressed amazement that in this group of men, "Political talent bloomed as if touched by some tropical sun."[13] Another declared, "We may be amazed, as well as grateful, at the spectacle of the intellectual and moral caliber of the men who took a hand in shaping the American political tradition."[14]

John Adams said of his own contemporaries, "The Art and Address, of Ambassadors from a dozen belligerent Powers of Europe, nay of a Conclave of Cardinals at the Election of a Pope, or of the Princes of Germany at the Choice of an Emperor, would not exceed the Specimens We have seen."[15] In England, the great William Pitt said before the House of Lords, "I have read Thucydides and have studied the master states of the world . . . no Nation or body of men can stand in preference to the General Congress at Philadelphia."[16]

This amazing group of men came together from disparate social, economic, and political backgrounds to accomplish something unique in history. They led the first revolt of colonies against a European power. While waging war, they created a political system to unify a group of colonies widely separated by geography, culture, economic interests, and religious affiliations. They took the concept of democracy beyond anything seen before. Unlike other revolutions to follow, their work endured the test of history.

Historians are only able to wonder at how such an amazing group of men came together. Arthur Schlesinger speculates about education, social mobility, and his belief that statecraft may have been the best outlet for men of ability at that time. He even alludes to "a lucky concatenation of genes." He finally concludes, however, "The mystery remains." Barbara Tuchman offers the suggestion that the demands of the time might have produced such men; that the founders were men responding to a unique opportunity to create a new political system. Yet she also states, "It would be invaluable to know what produced this burst of talent," and "The Founders remain a phenomenon to keep in mind to encourage our estimate of human possibilities."

Unfortunately, in this secular age, we are not surprised that historians and textbook writers overlook the obvious explanation of this phenomenon. This flowering of talent among the founders of America is, in my opinion, a manifestation of God's hand at work in the founding of this nation. In fact, I believe that we see revealed one of the clearest examples of God's action at any time or place in history.

The American founders were an interesting group of men with a wide range of talent and experience. Most acquired exceedingly good educations and broad knowledge of philosophy, classical law, and politics. Most came from Christian families. All showed a deep reverence for God, although several developed their own antipathies toward the religious organizations of the time. The unique individual talents of these men are amazing. Even more astounding, however, is the fact that somehow they came together at this critical moment in history. I believe that only God's hand could have assembled such a group and provided the courage, perseverance, and unity needed to accomplish a great purpose. These men had to conduct a war against the most powerful military establishment in the world and, at the same time, set a new nation on the course to greatness.

The following pages present brief biographical summaries of John Adams, Thomas Jefferson, Benjamin Franklin, John Witherspoon, and James Madison. A later chapter will address George Washington. These are the men who I consider most influential in conceiving and implementing the American Revolution. There were of course other great founders who could be included, but I do not believe that any of those addressed here could be excluded from such a list.

JOHN ADAMS

John Adams's vision and energy made him the most dynamic force in the Continental Congress. His single-minded effort led to the final separation from Britain and assured that he would be remembered as the architect of independence. Later his energy and vast knowledge of law and political history were vital to establishing the form of the new state and federal governments, all of which bear the imprint of his genius.

Adams was born in 1735 in Braintree, Massachusetts, to a solid farming family and pious parents. He was studious by nature and the first in his family to attend college. He went

Portrait of John
Adams (paint-
ing by Gilbert
Stuart—National
Archives)

to Harvard with the aim of becoming a minister but eventually learned that he had problems with church orthodoxy and
authority. He wrote in his diary, "Where do we find a precept
in the Gospel, requiring Ecclesiastical Synods? Convocations?
Councils? Decrees? Creeds? Confessions? Oaths? Subscriptions
and whole cartloads of other trumpery that we find religion
encumbered with in these days?"[17]

Unwilling to deal with the apparent rigidity of church doc-
trine, Adams began to pursue other professional interests. He
discovered an aptitude for law and politics and educated himself thoroughly in the classical literature of these fields. Highly
intelligent and ambitious, he built a solid legal practice in

Massachusetts. He also held a series of public offices and began to emerge as a leader of those opposing British measures infringing on colonial rights. He wrote essays, articles, and books addressing these issues and became an outspoken and controversial public figure.

His willingness to defend the British soldiers involved in the so-called Boston Massacre of 1770 gives a glimpse of his independent nature and integrity. When public opinion intimidated other lawyers from undertaking this unpopular task, he agreed to be the defense attorney himself. He put forward a masterful case and won acquittal for the officer and six of the eight men involved.

At the age of thirty-nine Adams went to Philadelphia to represent Massachusetts in the Continental Congress. His energy, strong opinions, and deep knowledge of political theory gave him great influence with the other delegates. Convinced by 1776 of the need to separate from Britain, he led the fight for independence within the Congress. In the final debate he gave the decisive summation and brought the issue to vote. Although Jefferson wrote the Declaration, Adams accomplished the fact of independence.

At the request of other convention delegates, Adams drafted an essay on the structure of a new government. This work was circulated and published as a pamphlet titled, *Thoughts on Government*. The essay began "It has been the will of Heaven that we should be thrown into existence at a period when the greatest philosophers and lawgivers of antiquity would have wished to live . . . How few of the human race ever had an opportunity of choosing a system of government for themselves and their children?"[18]

The challenge facing Adams and the other delegates was to devise a new government without hereditary nobility or recognized royal authority. Many felt that they would have to somehow create or simulate these European institutions. Adams, however, proposed an elected executive, two-part legislature, and independent judiciary. He carefully articulated the need for balance between contending components of government.[19]

Adams's views on the structure of government did not prevail for some time on the national level. With the war in progress, the states adopted Articles of Confederation in 1778, giving practically all power to the individual states. The states then became the forum of constitutional debate.

In 1779 Adams was elected to a convention in Massachusetts to develop its first constitution. Elected to the thirty-member drafting committee, he was then selected to a sub-committee of three. The other two members of that committee gave Adams the actual task of writing the state constitution for Massachusetts.[20]

Adams expanded his *Thoughts on Government* and developed a three-part governmental structure with executive, legislative, and judicial departments. He also wrote a Declaration of Rights, guaranteeing elections, free speech, and liberty of the press. Regarding religion, he provided that it was the duty of all people to worship the "Supreme Being, the great creator and preserver of the universe." He also included the provision that no one would be "hurt, molested, or restrained in his person, liberty, or estate for worshipping God in the manner most agreeable to the dictates of his own conscience."[21]

This document would become the model for practically every other state and eventually the federal government. As Adams's biographer, David McCullough, so eloquently states, "As time would prove, he had written one of the great, enduring documents of the American Revolution. The constitution of the Commonwealth of Massachusetts is the oldest functioning written constitution in the world."[22]

For almost ten years Adams served at diplomatic posts in Europe, gaining support during the war years and representing the nation's interests during the early years of peace. During the debate over the new constitution, he continued to write and to advocate a stronger federal government. He served as vice president to George Washington and was himself president from 1797 to 1801, successfully keeping the young nation safely on the constitutional course that he had charted. He and Thomas Jefferson died within minutes on the same day, July 4, 1826, exactly fifty years after their joint triumph of independence.

John Adams was one of the most deeply religious of the founders and yet was also highly influenced by the importance attached to reason by contemporary scientific and philosophical works. Today many would consider these incompatible positions. To Adams, however, there was no contradiction. He was personally convinced of the power of God's role in human affairs and also believed strongly that God gave him the ability to think for himself. He asserted the "divine right and sacred duty of private individual judgment."[23] For him, Christianity represented "the religion of reason, equity, and love; it is the religion of the head and of the heart."[24]

He exercised his own judgment in all things, whether in evaluating religious practices or the structure of government. While shunning dogma, he sought out valid first principles. He considered God to be the center of morality in that "There is no right or wrong in the universe without the supposition of a moral government and an intellectual and moral governor."[25]

Further, Adams believed strongly that the government he helped create could never be sustained without God. "Our constitution was made only for a moral and religious people. It is wholly inadequate for the government of any other."[26] Freedom was the foundation of the new nation, and Adams believed "it is religion and morality alone which can establish the principles upon which freedom can securely stand."[27] To John Adams freedom not centered on God was a prescription for disaster.

THOMAS JEFFERSON

Thomas Jefferson ensured his place in history by writing the Declaration of Independence. Others were the primary actors in the drama of the American Revolution, but he is credited with being the thinker. Highly intelligent, complex, and often tormented, his unique talents were important to the Revolution and especially critical in shaping the new government.

Jefferson was born to a solid Virginia family in 1743. From age nine to fourteen he lived away from his family under the tutelage of William Douglas, an Anglican minister who seems to have been a somewhat weak scholar and indifferent teacher. His father died when he was fourteen, and his education continued with another uninspiring Anglican minister, James Maury.

At William and Mary College Jefferson began to find the full scope of his intellectual interests under the supervision of Dr. William Small, a Scotsman and the only nonclerical member of the faculty. Small stimulated Jefferson's interest in mathematics and science. He was also notable for his criticism of the religious establishment and was influential in forming many of Jefferson's attitudes about religion.[28]

While officially studying law, Jefferson spent over six years at William and Mary pursuing a wide range of personal interests, including art, music, architecture, and philosophy. He was influenced greatly by the philosophers of the French and English Enlightenment. He read Locke, Montesquieu, Voltaire, and Diderot and grew to share their belief that only human reason and science could solve mankind's problems. He also shared

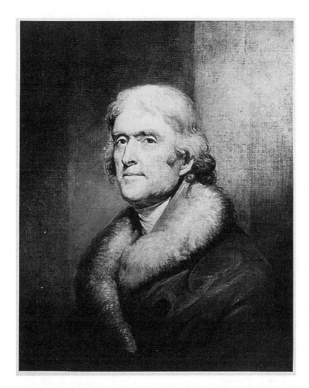

Portrait of
Thomas Jeffer-
son (painting
by Rembrandt
Peale—National
Archives)

the Enlightenment antipathy toward anything that restricted
scientific and philosophical inquiry. Jefferson grew increasingly
intolerant of church dogma and religious establishments that
demanded conformity of thought or practice.

In 1765 Jefferson was in the audience as the Virginia Assembly debated Patrick Henry's resolutions condemning the Stamp
Act, passed that year in England. During the next few years he
became more politicized by the conflict with England and was
himself elected to the Virginia Assembly in 1769. He was an
active member of the unofficial Committee of Correspondence,
coordinating resistance with the other colonies. Jefferson served
with George Washington in the Virginia Assembly of 1774.

The royal governor dissolved this group for going too far in its protests.

Jefferson attended the 1775 Continental Congress in Philadelphia, arriving at about the time of Washington's departure to take command of the military forces around Boston. Even though a military conflict was in progress, he absented himself for five months to return home to Monticello, to the consternation of many of the other delegates.

The thirty-three-year-old Jefferson returned to the Congress just in time for the climactic event of the era, the vote for independence. After Congress adopted the proposal of Richard Henry Lee on June 7, Jefferson was appointed junior member of a committee to draft a document announcing and explaining the actions of Congress. He was given the task of doing the actual writing mainly due to the fact that no one considered it particularly important at the time.[29]

Many of the phrases that Jefferson used came from George Mason's preamble to the Virginia Bill of Rights, which in turn owed much to John Locke's *Second Treatise on Government.* However, the Declaration of Independence had the imprint of Jefferson's own style and a uniquely timeless quality: "We hold these truths to be self-evident, that all men are created equal, that they are endowed by their Creator with certain inalienable rights, that among these are Life, Liberty, and the pursuit of Happiness."[30]

As the war heated up and activity in Congress grew busier than ever, Jefferson again returned to Virginia to take care of his affairs at Monticello. Declining an appointment to France, he instead attended the fall session of the Virginia Assembly where he involved himself in state legislative matters.

One of Jefferson's foremost achievements was doomed to initial failure. He poured himself into writing the Virginia Act for Establishing Religious Freedom, going farther than any other legislative initiative toward separating government and religion. His phrases were characteristically elegant: "Whereas Almighty God hath created the mind free; that all attempts to influence it by temporal punishments . . . are a departure from the plan of the Holy author of our religion, who being Lord both of body and mind, yet chose not to propagate it by coercions on either, as was in his Almighty power to do . . ."[31] It was then provided that "No man shall be compelled to frequent or support any religious worship, place, or ministry whatsoever, nor shall be enforced, restrained, molested, or burdened in his body or goods, or shall otherwise suffer, on account of his religious opinions or belief."[32]

The Virginia legislature rejected this bill for over ten years. Anglicanism remained strong in Virginia and the beneficiary of considerable state support. The religious establishment fought bitterly to defeat any encroachments on that support. Passage occurred in 1789 after a long fight and due to the successful political strategy of James Madison. As finally enacted, the Virginia Act for Establishing Religious Freedom became the model for religious provisions in many state constitutions and the U.S. Bill of Rights.

Thomas Jefferson's public career was long and distinguished. He served as governor of Virginia, ambassador to France, Washington's secretary of state, vice president, and then president of the United States. On most issues he was the voice of limited government, opposing measures to centralize power at the federal level.

Jefferson was a deep and complex man. Throughout a long public career his heart always seemed to be at Monticello and in his own thoughts and studies. He suffered much in his life, including the death of his wife in 1782, the deaths of children, extreme public criticism over his religious views, political muckraking over every aspect of his personal life, and chronic indebtedness. With his own travails in mind he made the lament to John Adams, "There are, even in the happiest life, some terrible convulsions . . . I have often wondered for what good end the sensations of grief could be intended."[33] Unfortunately, he found little comfort for his grief in the rational processes of his own intellect.

Thomas Jefferson was a great student of religion and an accomplished philosopher in his own right. He was a man of profound moral convictions and considered moral behavior to be the ultimate test of any religion or philosophy. On this subject he said, "It is in our lives, and not from our words, that our religion must be read."[34] He believed in the existence of a moral instinct and found it to be "the brightest gem with which the human character is studded."[35]

Jefferson saw in Christ's teaching the best basis for morality in the modern world in that "His system of morality was the most benevolent and sublime probably that has been ever taught, and consequently more perfect than those of any of the ancient philosophers."[36] "Had the doctrines of Jesus been preached always as pure as they came from his lips, the whole civilized world would now have been Christian."[37]

Despite his favorable view of Jesus Christ's moral teachings, Jefferson harbored a strong antagonism toward ecclesiastical authority and the established church. His opinions were the product of his educational experiences and a keen intellect. With his skepticism toward religious orthodoxy, he would fit the mold of many modern intellectuals. His devotion to reason and the efficacy of his own intellect precluded the possibility of any step of faith or spiritual experience in his life. He never found the comfort or peace that can come only from belief in a loving and personal God.

Thomas Jefferson's life and role in the American Revolution were no accident of history. This uniquely gifted man was a pre-eminent figure for over four decades at the focal point of developing constitutional thought. He applied his passionate love of freedom and antipathy toward tyranny to every aspect of government. He viewed Old World religious establishments as one of the foremost evils to be feared in America. If Jefferson and other key founders had been energetic and dedicated, church-supporting Christians, they could well have written Christianity into the fibers of American government. This was not God's plan for America.

Thomas Jefferson was used by God to achieve a great purpose. Unfortunately, dedication to his own ideals in pursuit of this purpose did not lead to a happy or peaceful life. He was never blessed with a personal faith that provided comfort during his tribulations or personal hope for the future.

BENJAMIN FRANKLIN

Considering his age at the time of the Revolution, Benjamin Franklin might be considered the grandfather of his country. When he signed the Declaration of Independence, he was seventy years old and clearly of an older generation than Washington, Jefferson, and the other founders described in this chapter. By this time in his life he was already a successful and famous writer, scientist, political figure, and diplomat. His prestige and good sense were invaluable to the Revolution and the new nation.

Franklin was born in 1706 to a large and pious household, and was baptized early into the Old South Church of Boston. As he grew up he observed prayer meetings in his own home, and his father expected him at one time to become a minister. As Franklin himself described it, "I was put to the grammar-school

Portrait of Benjamin Franklin (painting by Joseph Duplessis— National Archives)

at eight years of age, my father intending to devote me, as the tithe of his sons, to the service of the Church."[38]

Economic necessity required his service in the family business and the termination of his formal schooling after two years. After age ten Franklin was responsible for his own education, and he pursued it diligently by reading good books. He is a great example of a man able to benefit from a lack of school structure. He felt that learning was a lifelong enterprise and that no subject was beyond his interest or ability to learn. Apprenticed to his older brother in the printing business, he took that opportunity to develop and practice the writing skills that would be so important throughout his life.

By the time he was fifteen his studies led him into intellectual difficulty with the religious education of his Presbyterian upbringing. Some of the church literature arguing against dissent actually had the opposite effect on him and turned him for a time to deism.[39] Writing in his brother's newspaper, he made an indirect attack on what he saw in the church: "It has been for some time a question with me whether a commonwealth suffers more by hypocritical pretenders to religion or by the openly profane."[40] He later returned to belief in a personal God and acknowledged that "the kind hand of Providence . . . preserved me, thro' this dangerous time of youth."[41]

Although he gradually distanced himself from the organized church, Franklin's personal faith grew over the years. As he explained, "I never doubted . . . the existence of the Deity; that he made the world, and govern'd it by his Providence; that the most acceptable service of God was the doing good to man; that our souls are immortal; and that all crime will be punished, and virtue rewarded, either here or hereafter."[42]

At age seventeen Franklin went to Philadelphia where he eventually started his own printing business. His newspaper, the *Pennsylvania Gazette*, became successful, and he established papers in other colonies through partnerships with local printers. He became famous for his yearly collection of practical advice and weather information published as *Poor Richard's Almanack*, which by 1748 had become an institution, selling 10,000 copies a year. He became America's homespun philosopher with such enduring adages as: "Early to bed and early to rise makes a man healthy, wealthy, and wise." "Time is an herb that cures all diseases." "The rotten apple spoils his companions."[43]

Poor Richard's approach to religion was typically practical and sometimes cynical: "God helps them that helps themselves." "Many have quarreled about religion that never practiced it."

"Serving God is doing good to man, but praying is thought an easier service and therefore is more generally chosen." "None preaches better than the ant, and she says nothing."[44]

Franklin's interests practically knew no bounds. He became absorbed in the study of electricity, which was then a phenomenon of recent discovery and scientific inquiry. He read everything available on the subject and conducted his own experiments in his home. With the famous kite experiment he demonstrated the relationship between natural lightning and the static electricity produced in laboratories. He also conceived the use of lightning rods to deflect lightning from structures. Franklin's writings on electricity established his reputation as a scientist throughout the colonies and Europe. He was awarded honorary degrees by Yale, Harvard, and William and Mary, and elected to the Royal Academy and French Academy of Sciences.

Franklin's forty-year career as a public official began in 1751 with his election to the Pennsylvania Assembly. He soon led the fight against the Penn family proprietors in England over local control of matters affecting the colony. He went to England several times to represent Pennsylvania's interests. There he had the unique opportunity to acquire an inside view of English attitudes toward the colonies and to learn how difficult they would be to change. Over time, as his reputation grew and problems with England mounted, Franklin found himself speaking for all the colonies.

Appointed by the Crown to the position of Postmaster General in 1757, he turned his attention to completely reorganizing the postal service. He traveled throughout the colonies, systematizing procedures, surveying and selecting routes, and acquainting himself with local circumstances. He succeeded in speeding the mail and in further bringing the colonies together. Again, he seemed to involve himself in work that broadened his scope to the national level.

After the Stamp Act of 1765 ran into a storm of protest in the colonies, Franklin was again in England and was called before the House of Commons for the longest public appearance of his career. He plainly and forcefully presented the colonial point of view, frequently reminding the assembly that if they alienated America they risked more in trade than they would ever gain in taxes. Concerning the possible use of military forces, he observed prophetically that, "They will not find a rebellion; they may indeed make one." His testimony was recorded and published in England and America, and he was hailed a hero when the Stamp Act was repealed.

Franklin returned home in 1775 in time to be elected one of Pennsylvania's delegates to the Continental Congress. He became involved in practically every important matter dealt with by the Congress and brought his characteristic wisdom and humor to every duty. His personal prestige in the colonies and fame abroad were his most important contributions, giving credibility to the existence and actions of the Congress.

Franklin probably had more in common with Thomas Jefferson than any other delegate to the Congress, even though Jefferson was his junior by thirty-seven years. They were two philosophers among politicians, both quiet by nature with similar outlooks. Jefferson later observed, "I served with Gen. Washington . . . and Dr. Franklin in Congress. I never heard either of them speak ten minutes at a time, nor to any but the main point which was to decide the question. They laid their shoulders to the great points, knowing that the little ones would follow of themselves."[45]

In 1776 Franklin and Jefferson were paired together on the committee to draft the Declaration of Independence. Jefferson did the writing and Franklin the editing. Again, Franklin's foremost contribution was his involvement and prestige. His signature on the document was instantly recognized throughout America and

Europe. At age seventy the already famous writer and scientist added the title of revolutionary to his multifaceted resume.

In the late summer of 1776 the British invaded New York with overwhelming forces. The leaders of Congress had to face the reality of a long and difficult war. It was obvious that success depended on outside help. This task fell to Franklin, the one man who had already established a reputation in Europe and had proven himself a diplomat. He served throughout the war in France where his prestige grew further as a plain spoken and rustic hero of the Enlightenment. French economic and military aid did finally flow to America and were decisive in the war. Franklin made his own unique contribution to that success.

Franklin returned home in 1785 and was elected President of Pennsylvania. Two years later he undertook his last great mission. The Constitutional Convention convened in 1787 without clear legal standing and in an atmosphere of crisis. The eighty-one-year-old Franklin suffered from ailments and was not even able to stand. However, his mere presence gave legitimacy to the proceedings, and he used all his influence to create a climate of compromise and cooperation.

At a critical point in the debate on June 28, passions seemed to threaten a breakdown in the proceedings. Franklin appealed to a higher perspective and suggested a surprising strategy for the delegates: prayer.

> I have lived, Sir (speaking to Washington as president), a long time, and the longer I live, the more convincing proofs I see of this truth—that God governs in the affairs of men. And if a sparrow cannot fall to the ground without his notice, is it probable that an empire can rise without his aid? We have been assured, Sir, in the sacred writings, that "except the Lord build the House they labour in vain that build it." I firmly

believe this; and I also believe that without his concurring aid we shall succeed in this political building no better than the Builders of Babel. I therefore beg leave to move—that henceforth prayers imploring the assistance of Heaven, and its blessings on our deliberations be held in this Assembly every morning before we proceed to business.[46]

Benjamin Franklin was one of a handful who signed both the Declaration of Independence and the Constitution of the United States. His presence was critical to both. Just as he believed that God's hand shaped the affairs of nations, I believe that God shaped the life of this great man and placed him in the center of these events to ensure the success of the American revolution. Without him, failure would have been a distinct possibility at too many points to count.

JOHN WITHERSPOON

Of all the founders, Dr. John Witherspoon was probably the most overtly religious and, possibly for that reason, one of the least noticed in modern times. He came to America from Scotland in 1768 to become president of the College of New Jersey (later Princeton University). He was elected to the Continental Congress in 1776 and became one of the foremost leaders of the Revolution. He was the only college president and clergyman to sign the Declaration of Independence.

Witherspoon graduated from the University of Edinburgh at age seventeen and by age twenty-one was an ordained Presbyterian minister. Over the next twenty years his reputation grew as a preacher, minister, moralist, and published theologian. He became famous for his scholarly writing in support of Christian morality opposing many of the trends in philosophical thought current at that time. He was thoroughly familiar with the Enlightenment and placed high value on reason and free inquiry. Nevertheless, he believed strongly that reason could not compromise the gospel of Christ.[47]

At the College of New Jersey, Witherspoon found a young institution with firm roots in the Great Awakening. Founded by the Presbyterian Church in 1746, one writer described it as "the West Point of dissenting Presbyterianism."[48] After a rapid succession of presidents in the early 1760s, the trustees recruited Witherspoon as the ideal man to set the college on a new and lasting course. He brought his own powerful spiritual views and a solid academic background.

Witherspoon emphasized the development of civic as well as church leaders through a strong curriculum of science, economics, history, and philosophy. He did not hesitate to bring Enlightenment ideas into the classroom and encouraged his students to test their own faith against the new ideas that they were hearing. He personally saw no conflict between faith and reason, and believed that both were essential to a complete life. In his role as an educator, he stated, "Learning, without piety, is pernicious to others, and ruinous to the possessor. Religion is the grand concern to us all."[49]

Witherspoon's most profound influence on the Revolution stemmed from his firm grasp of the importance of religious freedom as the foundation of republican government. He believed that all human rights are based on one source: "the dignity of the free decisions each individual must make in the presence of the Creator."[50] The individual human being must make these spiritual decisions, and the freedom to do this is sacred and inalienable. He was convinced that freedom in society and civil government were necessary and supportive of this basic freedom.

Witherspoon drew the connection between civil and religious liberty from every period of history and concluded in one of his greatest sermons, "The knowledge of God and his truths have from the beginning of the world been chiefly, if not entirely, confined to those parts of the earth where some degree of liberty and political justice were to be seen . . . There is not a single instance in history in which civil liberty was lost, and religious liberty preserved entire."[51]

In the same sermon Witherspoon went on to say, "He is the best friend to American liberty, who is most sincere and active in promoting true and undefiled religion," and "God grant that in America true religion and civil liberty may be inseparable, and that the unjust attempts to destroy one, may in the issue tend to the support and establishment of both."

Witherspoon was highly influential in the Continental Congress, where he served throughout the war until 1782. He was a member of 120 committees and involved himself in practically every important issue. His personal accomplishments were only surpassed by his influence as an educator. He proved to be one of the most influential educators in American history. His students included a future president and vice president of the United States, nine cabinet officers, twenty-one senators, thirty-nine congressmen, three supreme court justices, and twelve state governors.[52]

JAMES MADISON

James Madison was John Witherspoon's star pupil at the College of New Jersey. However, historians have linked Madison most closely to his other mentor and role model, Thomas Jefferson. Madison's early life, education, and career paralleled Jefferson's, even though he was eight years younger and of a more practical nature. Both served in the Virginia Assembly, Continental Congress, and in the legislative and executive branches of the United States government. Madison is considered the father of

Portrait of James Madison (painting by Gilbert Stuart— National Archives)

the Constitution due to his singular accomplishment in bringing this foundational document into existence.

Madison was born in 1751, the oldest of eleven children, to an established, landowning Virginia family. His father built a simple but spacious mansion at Montpelier (within twenty-five miles of Jefferson's Monticello) that would be Madison's home all his life. He was baptized and raised an Anglican and attended the Brick Church where his father was a vestryman.

Like Jefferson, much of Madison's education was away from home and under the influence of Anglican ministers and Scottish scholars. At age eleven Madison was sent to school under Donald Robertson, a well-known teacher educated in Scotland. For five years he studied a well-rounded curriculum of mathematics, literature, geography, Latin, and Greek. He then returned home to continue school under his Anglican minister, Thomas Martin. Martin was a recent graduate of the Presbyterian-supported College of New Jersey at Princeton and was instrumental in steering his student there for the next stage of his education.

Madison's intellectual development progressed rapidly at Princeton under the influence of Dr. John Witherspoon, the college's president and primary teacher. Witherspoon taught classes to Madison in moral philosophy, rhetoric, and history. After graduating in 1771, Madison stayed at Princeton for another six months under Dr. Witherspoon to explore in depth the connection between civil and religious liberty. Witherspoon's attitudes toward religion and government took deep root within his student and would be a recurring theme throughout Madison's career.

At about this time Madison revealed concern for his own spiritual development while writing to a friend: "A watchful eye must be kept on ourselves lest while we are building ideal monuments of Renown and Bliss here we neglect to have our names enrolled in the Annals of Heaven."[53] In counseling the same friend about his decision to forgo a career in the ministry, Madison stated that the strongest testimony for religion would be for men of wealth and reputation "publicly to declare their unsatisfactoriness by becoming fervent Advocates in the cause of Christ."[54]

During his college years and after, Madison found himself caught up in the growing revolutionary temper of the time. From the beginning, however, he seemed to become more politically aroused over abuses within the Anglican Church than over issues of imperial authority. When officials in nearby Culpepper County jailed Baptist dissenters, he wrote passionately to his friend: "That diabolical Hell conceived principal of persecution rages among some and to their eternal Infamy the Clergy can furnish their Quota of Imps for such business . . . pray for Liberty of Conscience to revive among us."[55]

A few years later Madison put these sentiments into action. Elected to the Virginia Assembly in 1776, he was appointed to the committee charged with drafting a new constitution and declaration of rights for the state. He remained in the background during these proceedings, until the committee debated the article on religion. The draft proposal included words giving "the fullest Toleration in the Exercise of Religion." Madison honed in on the underlying assumption of this phrase, that there was a legally approved religion and that the state could decide to *tolerate* others. He successfully proposed a substitute clause with a profoundly different approach: "All men are equally entitled to the free exercise of religion, according to the dictates of conscience."[56]

Madison also made a proposal that to him logically followed the first, that "no man or class of men ought, on account of religion to be invested with peculiar emoluments or privileges."[57] This struck directly at the Anglican establishment in Virginia and was soundly defeated. As previously mentioned, Jefferson's Act for Establishing Religious Freedom met the same resistance, bonding these two men into a common cause for the future.

Madison was elected to the Continental Congress in 1779, serving for three years as its youngest representative. As the war continued, he experienced firsthand the problems inherent in the existing political structure. The government's fiscal condition was in shambles with mounting debt, rampant inflation, and insufficient funds even to pay the army. Madison led a small group that worked for a stronger central government and taxing power, but his efforts led only to frustration and disillusionment during this period.

Returning to the Virginia legislature in 1784, Madison teamed with Jefferson to reform the Virginia Constitution. He

was soon confronted with a legislative initiative by Patrick Henry
to impose a general assessment within the state to support Christian ministers of all sects. This bill had considerable Presbyterian,
Baptist, and Anglican support and appeared unstoppable. Madison used every tactic available to delay the bill while writing his
"Memorial and Remonstrance against Religious Assessments," a
powerful fifteen-point argument against the concept of the state
establishing or supporting religion.

Madison made his case pointedly: "During almost fifteen
centuries has the legal establishment of Christianity been on
trial. What has been its fruits? More or less in all places, pride
and indolence in the Clergy, ignorance and servility in the laity;
in both, superstition, bigotry and persecution. Enquire of the
Teachers of Christianity for the ages in which it appeared in its
greatest luster; those of every sect, point to the ages prior to its
incorporation with Civil Policy."[58]

Madison's document was published and circulated as a petition throughout the state. Due to his efforts and to Henry's
departure from the legislature (because of his election as governor), Madison was able to get the bill withdrawn. In 1786 he
used the initiative gained in this success to gain passage of Jefferson's Act for Establishing Religious Freedom. With great pride he
wrote to Jefferson, then in Paris, that they had "extinguished forever the ambitious hope of making laws for the human mind."[59]

During this period Madison continued to despair at the condition of government on the national level. Under the Articles of
Confederation the government still floundered financially, and
chaos was growing commercially as each state pursued its own
economic interests. He led the effort to convene a convention
in Annapolis to address common commercial problems. Only
five states attended the meeting, but it resulted in a request to
Congress for a full constitutional convention in 1787.

Madison prepared himself thoroughly for this moment in history. With Jefferson's help he amassed a library of the best works pertaining to law and the theory and history of government, from ancient and modern sources. He came to Philadelphia with more knowledge and focus than any other delegate, and he came with a plan.

Madison's Virginia Plan served as the basis for deliberation in the Convention. He sought a decisively stronger central government with power to tax and regulate commerce. Powerful executive and judicial branches were integral to his plan. Having seen the success of factional interests in countering the religious establishment in Virginia, he believed in the effectiveness of balanced power among contending branches of government, preventing one from tyrannizing another.[60]

Madison's genius went beyond creating the plan. He brought the energy and political skill to work the plan through four months of intense negotiations and compromise. When the delegates approved a final document in September, he immediately began the campaign for ratification. With Alexander Hamilton and John Jay, he contributed twenty-nine of a series of seventy-seven articles for the New York press that were collectively published as *The Federalist.* These became the classic and enduring commentary on the new constitution. The climactic ratification vote came in Virginia on June 25, 1788, establishing the Constitution of the United States as the foundational law of the land.

Madison's public career continued until 1817 and included service as Jefferson's secretary of state and two terms as president. He died in 1836, the last of the great "Founders." His legacy included volumes of journals and documents pertaining to his political life, but of all the founders, he left the least regarding his own religious experience.

We know that in his youth he studied theology and exchanged letters with a friend pertaining to his spiritual development. In his later life his approach to religion seemed to continue on a theoretical plane, as in this discussion: "The finiteness of the human understanding betrays itself on all subjects, but more especially when it contemplates such as involve infinity . . . the mind . . . finds more facility in assenting to the self-existence of an invisible cause possessing infinite power, wisdom, and goodness, than to the self-existence of the universe." He concluded, "The belief in a God all Powerful, wise, and good, is so essential to the moral order of the World and to the happiness of man, that arguments which enforce it cannot be drawn from too many sources."[61]

Like the other public figures presented in this chapter, Madison undoubtedly wanted to make sure that his public utterances not lean toward any religious persuasion. He had to carefully cultivate the habit of avoiding the issue publicly. Even so, his personal conversations or writings would have somewhere revealed any deeply held spiritual convictions. These seem not to exist in Madison's case. Perhaps his practical mind did not dwell on a subject that he could not figure out. Also, his lifelong battle against the structure of the church may have rendered him deaf to the message of the church.

Again, we see the miraculous nature of the American founding. Jefferson and Madison were the perfect men at this stage in history to ensure that a religious establishment would not become an integral part of the government of the new republic. God's plan for America was freedom, and the first freedom was to be found within the mind and soul of each citizen. A structure of state-supported religion would no longer cloud this freedom.

FOUNDING AMERICA

In Adams, Jefferson, Franklin, Witherspoon, and Madison we see a group of uniquely gifted men with extraordinary vision and talent. The great Founding Father, George Washington, is the subject of Chapter Four. Obviously, all of the founders have not been included. I have focused on the most well-known and most influential, and those who were deeply involved in events leading up to the revolution and the war itself.

The idea of independence did not come quickly or easily to any of these men. Motivated to varying degrees by ambition and civic-mindedness, each responded to the call to serve in his own colonial assembly and to oppose British oppression. They sought redress of their grievances as British subjects. Over time they were empowered to transcend disputes over taxation and to focus their attention and that of their countrymen on the higher question of freedom itself.

Somehow this unique group of men was able to integrate classical learning and modern concepts of philosophy with their own spiritual convictions and common sense. These were all religious men and conscious of the role of religion in supporting the moral fiber of the nation. God used this amazing talent to somehow blend the crosscurrents of the Great Awakening and the Enlightenment into a new civil and religious order unseen before in history. The structure of the church was separated from government. The freedom of the human conscience was enshrined as the cornerstone. Religion remained supremely important, but was not used to support the civil authority and was not itself manipulated by that authority. As events led from one crisis to another these amazing founders displayed an astounding ability to take the long view. They consciously conceived their place in history and their opportunity to create a new form of government for the ages.

CHAPTER THREE
LOSERS

"The retention of America was worth far more to the mother country economically, politically, and even morally than any sum that might be raised by taxation, or even than any principle so-called of the Constitution."

—EDMUND BURKE[62]

THE FOUNDING of America required men of outstanding character and vision. The other side of this coin, however, was the losing of America. Although there were many honorable men in British politics during the period of the American Revolution, it is a fact that they made disastrous mistakes and miscalculations at almost every turn. Unfortunately for Britain, her greatest men were not in power during these very important decades. I believe that we see here another miraculous pattern of events and grouping together of men at a critical time in history. This unfortunate group of British leaders seemed to work against their country's own interests as they presided over the loss of the American colonies.

Under George I and George II, the so-called Hanoverian kings, England achieved a remarkable stability during the early 1700s. Parliament brought George I to the throne from the German duchy of Hanover to ensure the continuation of Protestant rule. He spoke no English and relied heavily on the expertise of his ministers. Foremost among these was Sir Robert Walpole, who became in effect the first prime minister under George I and George II, serving to 1742. Both kings benefited from the continuity provided by this long tenure.

One feature of Walpole's administration was a benign neglect of the American colonies. This evolved from an overriding concern for free trade and commerce. Even though various laws were in effect setting tariffs and restrictions on manufacture in the colonies, enforcement was lax and smuggling was common. Regarding the issue of directly taxing the colonies Walpole stated, "No! It is too hazardous a measure for me; I shall leave it to my successors."[63] Time, distance, and Walpole's extended tenure all served to foster a separation between America and the mother country.

William Pitt was another remarkable political figure who served during the reign of George II. Pitt was a commoner who rose to influence in Parliament by his energy, forceful personality, and brilliant oratory. He entered the government in a minor post in 1746 and was elevated to secretary of state in 1756. He assumed leadership of the cabinet at a point when the Seven Years' War with France was going badly for England and her allies in Europe.

After acquiring almost unlimited war powers, Pitt masterminded a brilliant strategic campaign. Giving token support to his Prussian allies in Europe, he focused Britain's naval strength on France's seagoing commerce and foreign holdings, with the long-range goal of expanding Britain's trading empire. This campaign brought victories in Canada, the frontier of the American colonies, the Caribbean, and India. Horace Walpole called him, "the most successful genius that ever presided over our councils."[64] Unfortunately, those advising George II's grandson, the future king, viewed Pitt's success and growing power with suspicion.

GEORGE III

George III was the third king of the Hanoverian line. By all rights he should not have become king for another twenty years, but his father, Frederick, had died suddenly and unexpectedly in 1751 when young George was thirteen years old. His grandfather, George II, ruled until 1760 when he also died unexpectedly.

King George III (painting by Benjamin West— National Archives)

The accession of George III to the throne in 1760 was a pivotal event for the British Empire and America. If Frederick had lived to a normal age and become king, or if George II had lived a few years longer, the British government would have been far better prepared to deal with events during a critical time in British-American relations. Instead, a young, idealistic, and inexperienced man took the throne at age twenty-two.

George's main qualities seemed to be an earnestness to be a good king and a definite obstinacy in pursuit of whatever he decided was the right thing to do. Although well-educated, he was not gifted intellectually. One notable deficiency in his education was his isolation from contemporaries. This left him with an inadequate understanding of the people he would have to work with and contributed to a withdrawn nature and his seclusion as king. What he learned about life outside the court came mainly from books.[65]

When George was seventeen years old, John Stuart, the third Earl of Bute, was brought into the royal household as tutor. Going beyond his role as teacher, Stewart became a close friend, father figure, and eventually the focus of an almost neurotic attachment and dependence. Increasingly George began to formulate his political views on the advice of Stewart and his own mother. Both were convinced that scheming ministers and factions within the cabinet manipulated George II. This attitude would color George's approach to his own rule for years, as reflected in his cynical observation about the men who served him: "I look on the majority of politicians as intent on their own private interests instead of that of the public."[66]

With the unexpected death of George II on October 25, 1760, George III ascended to the throne. Showing unusual humility he assessed himself: "I do not pretend to any superior abilitys, but will give place to no one in meaning to preserve the freedom, happiness, and glory of my dominions, and all their inhabitants, and to fulfill the duty to my God and my neighbour in the most extended sense."[67]

The young king immediately appointed Bute to the cabinet and made it known that his tutor would be the power behind the throne. Together they began maneuvering to reform the government and to unseat Pitt and other key ministers. Although Pitt was the architect of the nation's amazing success in the war with France, he became the object of an almost irrational dislike on the part of the king and Bute. Unfortunately, this dislike and maneuvering for control seemed to include no corresponding political or strategic vision.

On Pitt's resignation from the cabinet in 1761, George looked to Bute to form a new government. At this critical juncture his friend and mentor failed him completely. Controversy was then raging over the war and peace negotiations with France. Bute backed away from this opportunity to exercise direct power and from the burden of direct responsibility. He stated, "The angel Gabriel could not at present govern this country but by means too long practiced and such as my soul abhors."[68] His academic knowledge unfortunately did not translate into actual political ability or character.

The disillusioned king had to turn elsewhere to find the men to form a new government. Over the next ten years he would have to deal with ever-changing combinations of ministers that could command majorities in Parliament and govern the nation. He found himself forced to work with those same schemers and factions that his tutors had taught him to abhor.

Historians describe the earlier Hanoverian regimes as having weak kings and strong ministers. The reign of George III tended to be the opposite, a strong king with weak ministers. Unfortunately, his strength was usually manifested in his stubbornness. He seldom admitted mistakes or yielded to any-one else's opinion. He felt that he was the only person acting with pure motives. In regard to Britain's vital relationship with the American colonies, the only issue that seemed to capture his attention was obedience to the Crown.

Between 1761 and 1770 turnover within the cabinet was constant and unlike anything seen before in Britain. At no time was there a constant or coherent vision in domestic or foreign policy. During this period the temperature in the American colonies was slowly heating to the boiling point, and no one in the government seemed to have a grasp of America's or even of Britain's long-term interests. One official would write, "The parliamentary cabals which divided the court during the first twelve years of George III, being mere struggles for favour and power, created more real blood and personal rancour between individuals than the great questions of policy and principle which arose on the American and French wars."[69]

GEORGE GRENVILLE

In 1763 the king formed a new ministry under George Grenville, appointed leader of the House of Commons and First Lord of the Treasury. Grenville was the brother-in-law of William Pitt and had served in minor government posts for twenty years. Breaking with Pitt, he allied himself with Bute and benefited from Bute's sponsorship to the top post. The king at this point was willing to deal with almost anyone except Pitt and specifically guaranteed Grenville that he would not call Pitt back into service. The one man capable of molding an effective government continued to be excluded from office.

Grenville's main qualities were an aptitude for hard work and a knowledge of finance. However, the well-being of his own family's finances often seemed to dominate his agenda, followed by a zeal to control all appointments and protect his own power. Both of these interests brought him into conflict with the king, who came to consider him greedy and of a "selfish disposition."[70] These traits were particularly abrasive to the young and idealistic George III and eventually ensured an active dislike for his first minister.

The Stamp Act was Grenville's great policy initiative, reflecting his focus on the nation's financial condition and war debts. He felt that the American colonies needed to pay more to reduce those debts and to support the cost of administering the newly acquired territories in North America. The act was proposed in 1764 and quickly engendered a storm of protest from the colonies and from their colonial agents in London. The act required the purchase of stamps for all printed legal and business documents and managed to affect and irritate practically every citizen of the colonies.

In spite of the protests, Parliament passed the Stamp Act in 1765 by the overwhelming vote of 249 to 49. This was the first direct tax levied on America. There was very little debate within Parliament and not even mention of the subject in correspondence between the king and Grenville.[71] Even though Grenville and his colleagues knew that the act was widely unpopular and would likely have a harmful effect on trade, they felt the need to assert their right to tax the colonies. Unfortunately, they did not foresee the vehemence of the American response. They were completely caught off guard when nine colonies came together to limit importation of British goods.

After a decline in trade of about one million pounds'[72] loud complaints from British merchants persuaded Parliament to repeal the Stamp Act in 1766. By that time the king had already removed Grenville from office on an unrelated issue, and the damage was largely done. Vast ill will and a new sense of common purpose had been implanted in America. As if to keep the wound open indefinitely, Parliament, under the Marquess of Rockingham, quickly moved to pass the Declaratory Act, proclaiming its authority undiminished to make future laws governing and taxing the colonies.

WILLIAM PITT

Rockingham's tenure as first minister was brief. His one notable achievement was repeal of the Stamp Act, which, unfortunately for him, involved bringing considerable pressure on the king. He then became involved in a dispute with the king over royal family finances, and this sealed the fate of the young marquess. In July 1766, disillusioned with Rockingham and unwilling to go back to Grenville, George III turned to the one man that he had sworn against. He called William Pitt to form the fifth government in the first six years of his reign.

At this point Pitt was fifty-eight years old and still the most dominant man in British politics. The "great commoner" continued to wield the power and the means to create a united and stable government. His reputation was strong in America where his success in the Seven Years' War was remembered, and his opposition role in Parliament was appreciated. Pitt quickly brought vision to the cabinet by proposing peace in America and a new continental alliance in Europe.[73] Unfortunately, he was not destined to realize the great potential of his administration.

Pitt was first victimized by his own ambition. He had long desired to become a member of the aristocracy and insisted on a peerage and seat in the House of Lords as conditions for taking power. The king granted these requests, and Pitt assumed the title Earl of Chatham. With this change in status he not only relinquished his dominant position in the House of Commons but also suffered an unexpected loss of respect and prestige with the public. This might not have been crucial except for another more serious problem.

In the winter of 1766 Pitt was struck down with the strange malady known as gout.[74] He was incapacitated to the point of being bedridden and had to leave London. His physical pain led to prolonged periods of sullen and even delirious behavior. Even though most physicians knew that diet and exercise would moderate the disease, Pitt's doctor believed in a different approach. He prescribed extra amounts of wine, normal consumption of red meat, and no exercise, attempting to drive out the illness through a violent fit of gout, according to the "theory of opposites."[75] It was a miracle that Pitt even survived.

Although he remained as the titular head of the cabinet, Pitt was not able to exert any sustained or consistent control of the government throughout 1767 and 1768.[76] Oversight of the cabinet fell to the thirty-one-year-old Duke of Grafton who proved to be totally out of his depth. The result was continued drift in government and more aggravation for America.

Charles Townshend, a cabinet member and influential figure in Parliament, stepped into this power vacuum. As Chancellor of the Exchequer he was able to propose monetary legislation. He used the opportunity to get back to what he and many in Parliament considered unfinished business: taxation of the colonies. Unfortunately for America, Townshend was a persuasive orator with a sympathetic audience.

On May 15, 1767, Parliament passed the infamous Townshend Acts by a vote of 180 to 98.[77] The acts assessed import duties on glass, lead, paint, paper, and tea products, all used widely throughout the colonies. They also created a new bureaucracy to enforce collection. A portion of the taxes was earmarked for payment of colonial officials such as governors and judges, in effect removing them from control of the elected colonial assemblies.

Only one year after repeal of the Stamp Act, Charles Townshend, a vindictive Parliament, and a supportive king thus ensured that there would be no rapprochement with America. The result was entirely predictable. Passions were reignited throughout the colonies. Over the next two years the colonists would cut their importation of British goods by over 30 percent.[78] The taxes raised would prove a fraction of this loss of trade and expense of a growing military presence.

Pitt's return to power presented one of the last great opportunities to reconsider the American problem. Due to the unusual circumstances of William Pitt's health and the malpractice of his doctor, this did not happen. The historian Barbara Tuchman wrote that, "Fate interfered . . . if Chatham had been healthy the history of America would have been different."[79] It is my belief that something other than "fate" was at work in these events.

FREDERICK, LORD NORTH

In 1767 Charles Townshend died suddenly of a bowel inflammation a few months after passage of his American legislation.[80] He was replaced as Chancellor of the Exchequer by the thirty-five-year-old Frederick, Lord North. In early 1770 the king called on North to form the sixth new government of his ten-year reign. As it turned out, the king finally got the stability in government that he had been seeking. North would serve for twelve of the most crucial years in British history. He and George III would forever be the British officials most identified with the American Revolution.

Lord North was an unusually amiable and likable man with a mild temper. He had served in Parliament since he was twenty-two, continually reelected from a family-controlled borough with thirteen voters.[81] Unfortunately, North experienced chronic financial difficulty and was often preoccupied with his own financial problems. At one point he accepted money from the king to settle his debts.[82] This was hardly a testament to the soundness of his judgment or his independence as a minister.

On practically every matter, North followed the wishes of the king. He had voted for the Stamp Act and against its repeal, and usually stood against conciliation toward the colonies. However, the economic problems brought on by the Townshend Acts had grown to crisis proportions, bringing intolerable pressure on Parliament for repeal of all the new duties imposed on America. North had to deal with this issue within a month of coming into office.

George III made his wishes known in a note to North: "I am clear that there must always be one tax to keep up the right, and as such I approve the tea duty."[83] With these marching orders North worked to repeal all of the Townshend duties except for one. Parliament retained the tax on tea to "keep up the right," and to cause more trouble in America.[84] The duty itself was bad enough, but the proceeds were used to pay the salaries of British officials in the colonies, depriving the colonial assemblies of one of their few controls over those officials.[85]

In all respects North proved to be the king's man. He seldom questioned George III's judgment or decisions. On matters of policy he seemed to have few opinions of his own, while working for a man full of opinions. North recognized his own limitations and frequently offered his resignation to the king.[86]

Regarding America, he inherited a certain momentum in events that he had neither the vision nor the strength to alter.

The king and many members of Parliament were becoming ever more antagonistic toward their rebellious "subjects" in America. Even though the tide of events was contrary to Britain's own self-interest, it would have taken a man of strong character to stand against it. Frederick, Lord North was not such a man.

GEORGE GERMAIN

One of North's biggest mistakes was appointing Lord George Germain to a critical cabinet post in 1775. During the Seven Years' War, Germain, formerly George Sackville, had served in the army as a cavalry general. A court martial had found him guilty of failing to lead a key attack in the Battle of Minden in 1759. He was dismissed from the service and declared "unfit to serve His Majesty in any military capacity whatsoever."[87]

In spite of his military failure, Germain held a seat in Parliament because of his connections to one of the oldest, most aristocratic families in England. He was highly energetic, hard-working, and a forceful public speaker. He was also caustic, vindictive, and ambitious. His political career prospered mainly due to his loyalty to the king.

Germain came into the North cabinet as a vigorous advocate of "bringing the rebels to their knees."[88] Many felt that he intended to wipe out the stain of Minden by conquering America.[89] As Secretary for the Colonies he was directly responsible for the war effort. For obvious reasons his military counterparts did not hold him in the highest esteem, and he returned the sentiment fully. Ironically, this man deemed "unfit to serve . . . in any military capacity" would exercise direct control over the British military high command during one of the most critical periods in its history.

LOSING AMERICA

During this era, leaders on both sides of the Atlantic made mistakes. Of the Americans it can at least be said that they usually acted in their own self-interest. The same cannot be said of the British. During the 1760s and '70s an unusual combination of small men and narrow minds set Britain's agenda. Budget deficits and revenue were the focus from the start. When resistance flared in the colonies, attention shifted to a search for more palatable forms of taxation. Continued resistance led to frustration and anger. Finally, obedience to royal and parliamentary authority became the focus of all concern. As one cabinet member put it, "If the King's authority is not on this occasion to be supported, there is an end of the British Empire."[90] Neither the king nor his key ministers showed the statesmanship to look beyond the protests to consider the American point of view or even Britain's own underlying interest.

As a great trading nation Britain's interest was undeniably commerce. Exports to America during this time were about 2.5 million pounds per year.[91] Compared to this economic activity the stamp tax was projected to raise at most 60,000 pounds. The Townshend duties brought in 16,000 pounds during their first year, as trade with America plummeted by 800,000 pounds.[92] Clearly Britain's interest was to nourish and increase trade with America. Instead, her statesmen seemed bent on risking its existence.

Many of these taxes were not unusually onerous, or even unfair. Several cabinet ministers observed that taxes are never popular. They believed that the Americans would eventually get over their grievances and get on with life as usual. Unfortunately, no British minister ever visited the colonies or listened carefully to the colonial representatives in England. The nature and extent of the growing anger in America were ignored.

Other solutions were available, but, unaccountably, were not seriously considered. The answer to "taxation without representation" was simple. Colonial representation in Parliament would have rendered America's objections completely invalid. Instead, the idea of virtual representation appeared.[93] Many convinced themselves that members of Parliament could speak for the colonies even if not elected by them.

Another solution would have been to have the colonies tax themselves. Various officials proposed this idea and saw it rejected several times. Lord North himself suggested it in 1775 as a conciliatory gesture, but by then it was too late to alter the course of events.

The most far-reaching solution to the problem would have been some plan of union or confederation. Benjamin Franklin was one of the few men of this era with the vision to think in these terms. He saw both the growth potential of the colonies and the depth of colonial loyalty to the British Crown. He studied ways to structure a relationship that would benefit both colonies and mother country. His proposed plan of union, like every other positive solution, received little attention.

The ineptitude in British government during this period derived from the men in power. These men were the product of a phenomenon later termed the "politics of maneuver."[94] The cabinet consisted of five to six ministers appointed by and supposedly loyal to the king. The king had to assemble this key group from one faction after another in shifting alliances. The energy of these men was centered on acquiring and holding on to power while attention to consistent policy goals suffered.

Unfortunately, men like William Pitt were the exception. The ruling class of the time came mostly from about two hundred families of noblemen with extensive interconnections in educational, social, professional, and family life. These privileged and wealthy owners of the great English estates involved themselves in government because they considered it their province. Government was the preferred employment and duty of gentlemen, and high government office allowed for the patronage of dependent relatives. This system obviously did not assure the best talent in key positions of authority.

GOD'S HAND

The account so far of the founders and losers reveals stark contrasts between the British and American leadership of the time. All acted to bring about one of the great events in history, the American Revolution. Those who believe in the randomness of history must at least wonder at the amazing collection of talent on one side and pervasive ineptness on the other. Within a few years after 1763 the unthinkable happened. Loyal subjects in the American colonies turned into revolutionaries, as an amazing group of far-sighted men seized on a new vision. Their vision was freedom, in accordance with z's plan for the new nation.

Many Americans during the 1700s, especially clergymen, considered America to be the modern-day "chosen people." They saw a "new Jerusalem," planted in the New World to carry God's kingdom to a higher level and to be a shining light to the rest of the world. It was possible then and now to see similarities between the struggling colonies and the story of the Israelites enslaved in Egypt during biblical times.

The book of Exodus tells how God brought freedom to the Israelites and formed them over time into a nation. An interesting aspect of the story is the part played by the Egyptian Pharaoh. In spite of repeated entreaties from Moses and repeated demonstrations of God's power through a series of plagues, Pharaoh would not let the Israelites go. In America's story, George III and his ministers played this role. America would never have come into existence as a nation without enduring many tribulations. The path had to be difficult, to forge a unity that had never before existed. The mistakes on the part of the British leaders had to be egregious to produce the strong reactions required to overthrow an existing political order. God used all of these men to achieve a great purpose.

Chapter Four
Founding Father

The young rider spurred his mount across the open field. The crack and concussion of rifle fire were constant and close. Much of it was aimed directly at him, the only officer in sight on horseback. Everywhere he looked he saw dead and wounded soldiers and shattered equipment. The formation of British regulars that had advanced with such precision an hour before was now disintegrating before his eyes. He felt another tug against his jacket and reached to feel if he was wounded. Suddenly his horse went down. Scrambling up in a daze he quickly found another. Horses were not hard to find as every other officer was now on foot. Exposure to this growing volume of well-aimed rifle fire was almost suicidal. Panic was beginning to ripple through the broken ranks. Back in the saddle, the rider returned to his self-appointed mission. He journeyed back and forth across the fire-swept field making contact with every unit, providing the only eyes and voice left to his severely wounded commander. Again and again bullets ripped his uniform coat. Another horse went down under him. On this day of chaos and death the young rider named George Washington amazingly survived. The twenty-three-year-old also found within himself a unique ability to focus fear and anger into a fierce determination. Twenty years later a great general would display these same traits on other battlefields as he changed the history of a nation.

O N JULY 9, 1755, young George Washington served as aide-de-camp to General Edward Braddock in this now obscure engagement of the French and Indian War. Washington not only survived this debacle in an amazing fashion, but also came out of it with an enhanced military reputation due to his heroism under fire. I believe that we can see the first miracle of the American Revolution in George Washington's survival on that day almost twenty years before the beginning of the Revolutionary War.

The greatest of the founders is the link between the men of part two and the battles of part three. He was a great political figure of the new nation, but he was first a soldier and architect of America's fight for independence. This man was the central figure in American military and political history for over fifteen years. It is difficult to imagine the founding of America without him.

THE YOUNG PATRIOT

Family. George Washington grew up in a respectable landowning family in northern Virginia and later inherited extensive landholdings in the region. His elder brother, Lawrence, was educated in England, but George attended small country schools in his early years and studied the subjects necessary to function in the world of agriculture and business. He was raised in the Anglican Church.

Between the ages of sixteen and nineteen, he journeyed frequently into what was then the western frontier between the Blue Ridge and Allegheny Mountains to survey the estates of the Fairfax family. His wilderness experiences helped build a strong self-reliance and independent mind, while his association with his brother Lawrence and the Fairfaxes helped refine his demeanor as a gentleman.

Early Military Experience. In 1751 Lawrence used his political influence to obtain an appointment for George as

George
Washington
as a Young
Officer
(painting
by C. W.
Peale—
National
Archives)

adjutant general of one of Virginia's military districts. He then
helped train his brother, aged nineteen, in the rudiments of sol-
diering. George's military aptitude and knowledge of the frontier
put him in a unique position to serve Virginia.

In 1754 Washington was the key figure in a military action
which historians consider the beginning of the French and
Indian War. The governor of Virginia sent him westward into
the Ohio River valley to support construction of a fort near the
site of present-day Pittsburgh. The French were also trying to
establish control of this region and had already occupied the
site, naming it Fort Duquesne. After several small skirmishes,

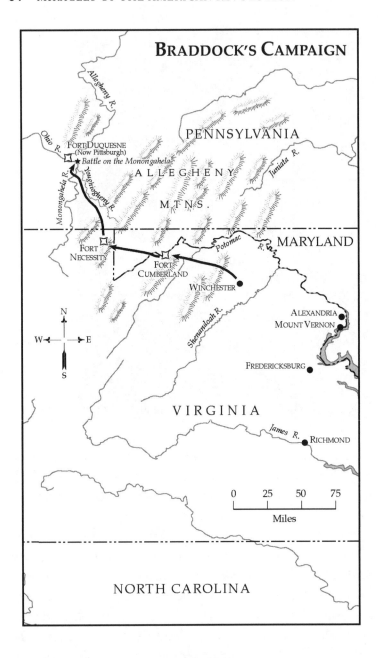

BRADDOCK'S CAMPAIGN

a larger French force attacked Washington and his unit, forcing their surrender. His opponents then allowed him to march out of the area and back to Virginia with his unit and reputation somewhat intact. He soon resigned from active military service and returned to Mount Vernon.

To counter the French threat west of the colonies the government in England dispatched Major General Edward Braddock and two regiments of regular troops to America. Braddock arrived in Virginia in 1755 to organize a campaign against Fort Duquesne. Due to Washington's experience in the area, Braddock gave him a staff position as an aide-de-camp.

On July 9, 1755, Washington experienced his second disaster on the Ohio frontier, mentioned already at the beginning of this chapter. After a three-month struggle through the Allegheny wilderness, Braddock was finally able to reach a point threatening the French fort. His army was superior to the defenders in every way except tactics.

Disdaining the use of his accompanying Indians as scouts, he deployed his army in formal array and ordered it forward. He walked into an ambush at a point about seven miles from the fort on the east bank of the Monongahela River. French troops supported by their own Indian allies opened fire from concealed positions. Well-aimed fire from this unseen enemy broke Braddock's formations. As the losses mounted, panic spread among the British troops. The British officers tried valiantly to gain control but suffered catastrophic casualties among their own ranks, including General Braddock and both of his British aides. Of eighty-six British and colonial officers on the field, sixty-three were killed or wounded in this ferocious fight.

Washington assumed the task of delivering the general's orders and receiving reports from every part of the battlefield, moving about openly on horseback. He was soon the only mounted officer left on the field, although enemy fire shot two of his horses from under him. He later discovered four bullet holes in his own coat. In a book titled *The Bulletproof George Washington*, David Barton examined this incident in great detail and included reports of those who repeatedly had Washington in the sights of their rifles. They and Washington believed strongly that on that day, "the all-powerful dispensation of Providence" protected him "beyond all human probability."[95] Even his military reputation managed to survive another disastrous defeat.

Colonial Politics. At the conclusion of the war, Washington again resigned his commission so that he could return home to Mount Vernon and the concerns of his family and estate. His public career continued, however, with his election to the Virginia Assembly, where he found his attention drawn inexorably to the growing conflict between England and the colonies.[96]

George Washington opposed the taxes and other offensive measures enacted by the British parliament. He supported restriction of trade with Britain as the best nonviolent option for resistance open to the colonies. This stand was not in his personal best interest. As an aristocratic planter he had close business ties with London, and anything affecting trade with England would strike at his own pocketbook. He was referring to himself when he wrote his friend George Mason, "I can see but one class of people . . . who will not or ought not, to wish well of the scheme—namely, they who live genteelly and hospitably on clear estates. Such as these, were they not to consider the valuable object in view and the good of others, might think it hard to be curtailed in their living and enjoyments."[97]

Early in 1769 George Washington himself rose in the opening session of the Virginia Assembly to present a series of resolutions highly critical of the British government. The assembly adopted the resolutions, and the governor found them so offensive that he immediately dissolved the body.[98]

Within a few years Washington's political career moved to a new level. He chaired a committee in his home county to define the position of his Fairfax constituents. He successfully presented resolutions to address dissatisfaction with Britain on the issues of representative government, taxation, and dissolution of assemblies. He affirmed the need for unity among the colonies with respect to cooperation and nonimportation of British goods. Washington presented these resolutions to a provincial meeting in Williamsburg that adopted them in essentially the same form. The delegates then appointed him and six others to represent Virginia at a General Congress of the colonies in Philadelphia.

Washington and delegates from the other colonies arrived in Philadelphia on September 5, 1774, to open the Continental Congress. His sentiments at this time are summed up in a letter to Bryan Fairfax: "I shall not undertake to say where the line between Great Britain and the colonies should be drawn; but I am clearly of the opinion, that one ought to be drawn, and our rights clearly ascertained."[99] Washington's agenda and his own character proved to be extremely influential. Patrick Henry commented, "If you speak of solid information and sound judgment, Colonel Washington is undoubtedly the greatest man on that floor."[100] The momentous meeting lasted fifty-one days and achieved a remarkable unity of action for such disparate individuals representing such widely varying interests.

THE WARRIOR

Growing Conflict. During the fall and winter of 1774–75 the prospects of military confrontation began to increase. Tension around Boston grew daily as General Gage, the newly arrived

British governor, deployed forces in and around the city and carried out his orders to shut down the port. With every indication that the military intended to enforce the unpopular edicts of Parliament by force, the local populace began mobilizing to resist. Volunteers calling themselves "minutemen" flocked to militia units throughout the region as military drills took on a new urgency.

Similar activity began to stir the colonies to the south. In Virginia the independent militia companies began calling on George Washington for instruction and advice. He traveled extensively to inspect and review preparations. Mount Vernon took on the tone of a military headquarters. As Washington prepared to travel to Philadelphia for the second Congress, even more disturbing news arrived from New England.

During the night of April 18–19, 1775, General Gage sent an expedition out of Boston to confiscate military stores and to arrest dissident leaders. Gage's troops exchanged small arms fire with local militiamen at Lexington and Concord. Eight colonials were killed. As the British units began their move back to Boston, other militia units arrived on the field to engage the British and to harass their extended column. Both sides suffered more casualties. At the end of the day, the British force was back in Boston confronted by a swelling array of colonial militia around the outskirts of the town.

The second Continental Congress convened on May 10, 1775, in an atmosphere of crisis. Military matters dominated the agenda, and Washington soon found himself chairman of the committees dealing with military issues.[101] Congress adopted his proposals for defense of the colonies, including the provision of arms, supplies, and forts.

In early June an appeal came from Massachusetts that the militia forces surrounding Boston be adopted by the Congress as an "American" army. The New England delegation knew how critical this proposal was to their own fate. They faced an uncertain future in their local conflict with Britain unless other colonies joined the effort. Many objected to such an overt widening of the military confrontation since they still hoped for reconciliation with Britain. The issue of who would command such an army became a crucial part of the debate.

Commander in Chief. Many felt strongly that a New England army would need a New England commander, and in fact already had one in General Artemis Ward. There was some support for British-born Charles Lee who had military experience in Poland. Many of the southern delegates favored George Washington, although his support was not unanimous. Edmund Pendleton of Virginia was well aware of the disasters in Washington's previous military career.[102]

John Adams saw that Washington's selection would firmly commit Virginia to what had been a New England struggle. Thanks in large measure to his persuasive efforts, the Congress acted on June 15, 1775, to adopt the forces around Boston as the Continental Army with George Washington as commander in chief. This action enabled Adams to achieve his aim of broadening the base of the conflict.

Washington referred to his appointment in these words: "An honor I neither sought after, nor desired, as I am thoroughly convinced that it requires greater abilities and much more experience than I am master of."[103] To his wife he wrote, "I shall rely confidently on that Providence which has heretofore preserved and been bountiful to me."[104]

On June 21, Washington and a small cavalcade left Philadelphia for Boston. After a brief ceremony with the Massachusetts Assembly, he continued on to Cambridge where he took formal command on July 3. In his first General Orders, issued on July 4, he stated his expectation "of all Officers and Soldiers, not engaged on actual duty, a punctual attendance on divine Service, to implore the blessings of heaven."[105] With reliance on God's help he shouldered a burden that he would not put down for eight years.

George Washington was a compromise choice to lead the military effort against England, and he had his own reservations about his capabilities. In retrospect it is difficult to imagine the selection of anyone else. Acts of personal heroism in combat and his long involvement with the Virginia militia formed the basis of his military reputation. His commitment to the cause of resistance was deep and well known. Everyone also knew that he had as much or more to lose than any other man in the colonies. He would eventually prove himself to be one of the greatest commanders in history.

Challenges. Washington's greatness as a military leader can be seen in the extent of his difficulties. To oppose the well-trained and equipped regular armies of Great Britain, he had to organize militia volunteers from throughout the colonies, with varying habits, loyalties, and skills. In an early report to Congress he stated, "It requires no military skill to judge of the difficulty of introducing proper discipline and subordination into an army, while we have the enemy in view, and are in daily expectation of an attack."[106] Adding to the difficulty was the fact that many units consisted wholly of men from particular towns and regions. They vehemently opposed the assignment of "outsiders" to their ranks. Efforts to change or standardize such procedures met stiff resistance.

Unlike his enemies, Washington never had the luxury of regular sources of arms, supplies, or money. The army was chronically and severely under-equipped and underpaid. Small arms and powder were especially critical. Winter clothing and material for shelter were almost nonexistent as the New England winter advanced.

Throughout the war Washington had to keep his own fears and frustrations largely to himself. In correspondence and in private meetings he complained bitterly to Congress. However, he was always understanding of Congress's plight. He never challenged or tried to undermine civilian authority. He felt that he could never afford to publicly complain about his difficulties. He was always vulnerable and afraid that his enemies would exploit any information about his own adversities. At every stage of the war, he had to carefully husband his resources and focus his strength for any operation against the enemy.

Of all his problems the most immediate and recurring had to do with the enlistments of his men. The minutemen around Boston had responded to the call of alarm at a moment's notice. They were equally prone to go home at a moment's notice when they perceived their duty done. The different colonial units had different ideas about their terms of service. The Connecticut men had agreed to serve until December 10, and on that date most actually did walk away from the battlefield. The other New Englanders considered December 31 to be the end of their service. In every unit absences were common due to sickness or urgent business at home.[107]

In one of the greatest and least recognized feats of military history, Washington and his officers organized a new Continental Army literally under the guns of the British forces concentrated in Boston. They worked tirelessly to enlist men and units for one year of service through the end of 1776. This required a tedious and difficult process of persuasion and cajoling. One year seemed then like a long time, but even a year would eventually prove woefully inadequate to the task of building a professional army.

Reporting to Congress, Washington described his plight, "It is not in the pages of history, perhaps, to furnish a case like ours. To maintain a post within musket-shot of the enemy, for six months together, without powder, and at the same time to disband one army, and recruit another, within that distance of twenty-odd British regiments, is more, probably, than ever was attempted. But if we succeed . . . I shall think it the most fortunate event of my whole life."[108] By December Washington had enlisted only five thousand men and throughout the winter his army teetered on the verge of dissolution. At one point he confided to a friend, "If I should be able to rise superior to these and many of the other difficulties . . . I shall most religiously believe that the finger of Providence is in it, to blind the eyes of our enemies."[109]

Washington himself was the key to eventually overcoming these difficulties. Even though his formal military background was not extensive, his strength of character and self-discipline were evident. He commanded authority and used it carefully. He insisted on the toughest standards possible under the circumstances. His approach to leadership and discipline were not complicated: "Require nothing unreasonable of your officers and men, but see that whatever is required be punctually complied with."[110] Above all else, he implored his officers to "impress upon the mind of every man, from the first to the lowest, the importance of the cause, and what it is they are contending for."[111] It was obvious to all that the flame of devotion to that cause burned within him.

Risks. During his military career George Washington placed himself in many dangerous situations, risking capture, wounds, and death. His fearless actions and miraculous survival under Braddock in 1755 were presented earlier in this chapter.

During his years of service in the Revolutionary War he continued to move about the battlefield with little regard for his personal safety. Several of these occasions will be mentioned in part three.

Washington probably came closest to death in an incident near Germantown, Pennsylvania, in September 1777. The British were advancing on Philadelphia, and the two armies were drawing close to each other along the Brandywine River. On September 7, Captain Patrick Ferguson of the British army was scouting with three of his men near Chadd's Ford.[112] Ferguson sighted two enemy officers on horseback a short distance away, well within range of the rifles carried by himself and his men. Before he could fire, the horsemen turned away and began moving away from his position. Ferguson described his next action himself: "It was not pleasant to fire at the back of an unoffending individual who was acquitting himself coolly of his duty, and so I let him alone."[113] Later Ferguson learned that the man who he had let live was General George Washington. Miraculously, Washington's life had again been spared, this time by the split-second decision of a young British officer.

Washington commanded the Continental Army throughout the Revolutionary War, from Boston to Yorktown. His continuity in this role was vital to the war effort and to the unity of the new nation after the war. On every occasion the American commander gave credit for his survival and success to God. After his greatest victory at Yorktown, he issued General Orders directing that divine services be held throughout the army to express the "gratitude of heart which the recognition of such reiterated and astonishing interpositions of Providence demand of us."[114] Part three will present more of Washington's actions during the major battles of the war.

Portrait of George Washington (painting by Gilbert Stuart— National Archives)

THE SOLDIER PATRIOT

Uncertain Peace. After Yorktown the struggling new nation entered a difficult and dangerous time. Hostilities seemed to be ending, but the politicians had not concluded a formal peace. Washington felt strongly that the time had not arrived to reduce military strength or vigilance. He argued his views strongly to a Congress growing in apathy toward military expenditures. After six years of war, the national treasury and foreign credit were practically exhausted. Without the power to tax, Congress could only requisition support for the army from the states. At this stage of the war, the states were reluctant to comply.

As this twilight period of apparent peace continued, the army itself experienced increasing turmoil. Many had enlisted for the duration of the war. They now felt that the war was over, and it was time to go home. The revolution had taken its toll on these men. In addition to the constant danger and family separations, there had been chronic shortages in supplies and money. Not only were there arrears in pay, but promises had also been made that veterans would receive pensions after the war. The likelihood seemed remote that the government would honor these obligations.

Crisis in the Army. As the months of 1782 wore on, suspicion grew within the ranks that no one would address their grievances. It was also apparent that the army's power to resolve these complaints would disappear once the army itself was disbanded. Anger and frustration built up, and rumors of revolt and mutiny began to spread. Washington received a letter from one of his senior officers stating that the army's ills were due to the new nation's republican form of government.[115] A dictatorship or monarchy under George Washington held a strong attraction to many. Dissidents circulated papers through the army calling for strong action against the political authorities while the power of the army was still strong. These events led to one of the defining moments in the life of George Washington and the United States.

At the peak of this dissension Washington called a meeting of all his field grade officers and representatives from every company of the army. On March 15, 1783, he walked alone into a packed and tension-filled room. For the first time in eight years he was not leading his men in a great cause, but was facing them as a potential adversary. With a remarkable speech he turned the tide of sentiment just as he had so often turned the tide of battle. He rightfully identified himself closely with the concerns of every man of the army. He explained the political process and all its delays. He reminded them of what they had accomplished in fighting for a new nation and that they were all now citizens of it themselves. He put himself at their command to represent their interests.

At one point he brought out a letter, and, after a hesitation, made the poignant remark, "Gentlemen, you will permit me to put on my spectacles, for I have not only grown gray but almost blind in the service of my country."[116] Tears flowed freely as the assembled officers voted unanimously to stand with their great leader and to forego a confrontation with civilian political authority. If Washington were a man with other personal ambitions, he could have easily led his army in an entirely different direction. How many times in history have successful generals used situations such as this to install themselves in power?

Peace. After lengthy negotiations the diplomats concluded the Treaty of Paris in January 1783. Upon receiving instructions from Congress, Washington issued General Orders declaring a cessation of hostilities at noon on April 19, the eighth anniversary of the first military action at Lexington. He directed that the orders be read to every unit in the army, to be followed by religious services to give thanks to "Almighty God for all his mercies."[117] His final orders to the army dated November 2 also expressed gratitude to God: "The singular interpositions of Providence in our feeble condition were such, as could scarcely escape the attention of the most unobserving—where the unparalleled perseverance of the Armies of the United States . . . for the space of eight long years was little short of a standing Miracle."[118]

Washington experienced an outpouring of emotion during his last days as commander in chief. He reentered New York City for the first time since his retreat seven years earlier, leading a formal procession of military and civilian authorities in public celebrations. After an emotional farewell with his officers he departed for Annapolis on December 4. As he passed through New Jersey, Pennsylvania, and Maryland, public officials greeted him, and well-wishers hailed him continuously.[119] He finally stood before a grateful Congress in Annapolis on December 23, 1783.

Once again, the most powerful man in America showed his lack of ambition for power and his own devotion to the subordination of military to civil authority. He resigned his commission, saying, "I consider it an indispensable duty to close this last solemn act of my official life by commending the interests of our dearest country to the protection of Almighty God. Having now finished the work assigned me, I now retire from the great theater of Action."[120] He returned to Mount Vernon to celebrate Christmas and to pick up the pieces of his personal life and family business.

General Washington Resigning His Commission (painting by John Trumbull—U.S. Capitol Rotunda)

THE POLITICAL PATHFINDER

Fortunately for America, George Washington's retirement did not signify a lack of interest in the progress of the new nation. Concerning its citizens he wrote, "This is the moment when the eyes of the whole world are turned upon them."[121] His concern continued that the new nation might lose what it had fought so hard to obtain.

Constitution. Problems were becoming more acute due to the lack of effective power at the national level provided in the Articles of Confederation. An amendment to levy a federal tariff on trade had failed. Federal and state debts were massive and many legislatures were not paying them. The war veterans themselves were the largest group of claimants. A revolt broke out in New England over land taxes and debts, threatening civilian authority at the state and federal levels. The states were implementing treaty provisions differently, and individual state laws on taxation threatened to overburden interstate commerce.

In 1786 a proposal was made for a convention of all the states to address these issues. There was wide interest in such a meeting, as many knew that substantial changes to the Articles of Confederation were under consideration. There was a problem, however, in that such a meeting had no standing under the Articles, and many considered it to be illegal.[122] There was one man who could give legitimacy to such proceedings.

Virginia elected Washington to head its delegation to the meeting, but he was reluctant to accept such an appointment. He had his own business interests and had also made a pledge to step down from public office. However, his sense of duty worked to draw him into this new struggle.

The open challenge to elected authority in New England concerned him. He wrote to his friend Henry Knox, "After what

I have seen . . . I shall be surprised at nothing, for, if three years since, any person had told me that there would have been such a formidable rebellion as exists at this day against the laws and constitution of our own making, I should have thought him a . . . fit subject for the mad-house."[123]

To many, insufficient power at the national level meant that one thing was lacking—a king. This sentiment was outrageous to Washington, even though he would have been the one viable choice for the position. He wrote John Jay, "I am told that even respectable characters speak of a monarchical form of government without horror. What a triumph for the advocates of despotism to find that we are incapable of governing ourselves, and that systems founded on the basis of equal liberty are merely ideal and fallacious!"[124] Perceiving these threats to the new nation and with no ambition for power himself, he finally consented to attend the convention.

Once assembled in Philadelphia on May 25, 1787, the delegates voted unanimously that George Washington chair the proceedings. Once selected, he exercised the authority of this position with careful restraint. He supported the Virginia proposal formulated by James Madison, but he seldom spoke publicly and managed to hold himself removed from most of the political infighting. He maintained cordial relations with most of the delegates throughout four months of exhausting negotiation and frequently heated debate. His most vital contribution to the new constitution was the fact that he associated his name with the convention and its final product.

There was no doubt in Washington's mind that God's hand continued to influence the new nation's destiny. In a letter to Lafayette he proclaimed it "little short of a miracle" that all the diverse interests represented at the convention could have come together to produce such a document.[125] Of the whole process he said, "We may, with a kind of pious and grateful exultation, trace the finger of Providence through those dark and mysterious events." With a warning for generations to come, he expressed confidence that the new government would prevent oppression "so long as there shall remain any virtue in the body of the people."[126]

By mid-September the convention had finished its work. Thirty-eight delegates signed the document and sent it to Congress. Four months of semisecret debate would explode into a yearlong public controversy as each state dealt with the question of ratification. His duty fulfilled, George Washington once again happily retired to Mount Vernon to resume the cares of his business and family life.

From Mount Vernon Washington followed developments in the ratification debates from a distance. He let his name be used by Madison and others, and he corresponded actively in support of ratification. Again, his primary contribution was the fact that his own signature was on the document. Also, as the debate progressed over powers of the newly created executive, there was the unspoken assumption that Washington himself would be the man to fill this post. This defused much of the central argument against the new constitution, that it concentrated too much power at the federal level.

President. By June of 1788 ten states had ratified the Constitution and thus assured its adoption. Presidential electors unanimously elected George Washington president in early 1789. In his first inaugural address Washington focused on God to express the thanks of a grateful nation, to ask his continued blessing, and to implore all to keep God at the center of the nation's business. Remembering all that God had already done, he said, "No people can be bound to acknowledge and adore the invisible hand, which conducts the Affairs of men more than the People of the United States. Every step, by which they have advanced to the character of an independent nation, seems to have been distinguished by some token of providential agency."[127]

It is hard to imagine a more perfectly suited man stepping forward at this stage of history to guide the republic through its early years. Every act set a precedent, and every decision formed a pattern for the future. At every turn Washington made the survival of representative government his guidepost. His personal prestige was his most valuable asset and was also the most valuable asset of the nation. He used it carefully, at times confounding both his supporters and adversaries by avoiding much of the political infighting.

Political passions in the young nation were strong and divisive as political parties quickly evolved to represent different views. The Federalists, under Hamilton, sought a stronger central government and favored friendly relations with England. The Republicans, under Madison and Jefferson, championed limited government and leaned toward France. The continuing controversy dismayed Washington, but he succeeded in a great balancing act for the sake of the nation.

Thanks mainly to Washington's personal authority, the government resolved critical issues during his administrations. He clearly established the extent of the new federal authority by his forceful and careful handling of the so-called Whiskey Rebellion. He presided over the great compromise addressing federal finances, debt consolidation, and location of the capital. He steered a balanced course between England and France, making sure that the United States did not come under the control of either. He endured his share of political abuse and criticism and was disheartened by all-to-frequent personal attacks. He worked through and endured the political process, with no recorded thought of solving his problems by usurping additional powers. It is difficult to imagine another man who could have held the new nation together through these crucial years.

Washington was elected unanimously to a second term in 1793 and could have easily been elected again. His final and greatest service was his refusal to serve a third term. The most powerful man in America again relinquished his power. He supervised the orderly and democratic process to replace himself and openly supported the new government. King George III of England said that these acts "placed him in a light the most distinguished of any man living."[128]

In his Farewell Address, he again called the nation to God: "And let us with caution indulge the supposition, that morality

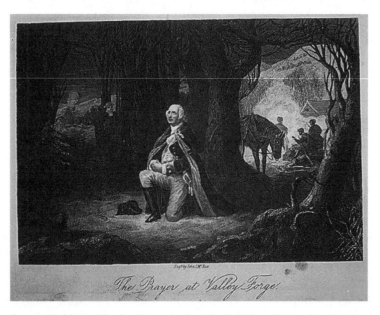

George Washington Praying (engraving by John C. McRae—National Archives)

can be maintained without religion . . . reason and experience both forbid us to expect that National morality can prevail in exclusion of religious principle."[129] Interestingly, many modern textbooks tell us that Washington's final address spoke to unity at home and neutrality abroad, ignoring this appeal to keep religion uppermost.

THE SPIRITUAL GUIDE

The nature of George Washington's personal religious belief has been the subject of scholarly investigation for over two hundred years. Historians have pretty well established certain facts. He was born, raised, married, and active all his life in the Anglican (later Episcopal) Church. He attended religious services faithfully and brought God into most of his public discourse and much of his correspondence.

Early biographers assumed that he was unquestioningly Christian and were able to cite many sources to confirm this view. In General Orders to the Continental Army he stated, "The General hopes and trusts, that every officer and man, will endeavor so to live, and act, as becomes a Christian soldier."[130] He said in a letter to the governors, "I now make it my earnest prayer that God . . . would be most graciously pleased to dispose us all to do justice, to love mercy, and to demean ourselves with that charity, humility, and pacific temper of mind, which were the characteristics of the Divine Author of our blessed religion."[131] Addressing a group of Delaware Indian chiefs in 1779 he made the statement, "You will do well to wish to learn our ways of life, and above all, the religion of Jesus Christ."[132]

Many modern biographers have chosen to paint Washington in a more non-spiritual light, linking him with the general deism of Thomas Jefferson and the ambivalence toward Christ shown by Benjamin Franklin. These writers believe that Washington's public and private references to Jesus and to his own faith were so few as to show a lack of spiritual conviction on his part.

These interpretations are possible because Washington himself was very private in most areas of his personal life, especially his faith. He once wrote, "In politics as in religion, my tenets are few and simple."[133] I have been frustrated in my own search for genuine expressions of Washington's personal faith. I conclude that he was probably the prototype of Episcopalians often encountered today. Many are personally and privately faithful but are not prone to talk about it.

In addition to his private nature, Washington also cultivated an ingrained objectivity as a national military and political leader. He felt that religion was best served by ensuring that government favored no religion. Leaders of practically every religious group approached him seeking assurance of how they would fare under the new government. His replies are instructive:

To the Baptists: "No one would be more zealous than myself to establish effectual barriers against the horrors of spiritual tyranny . . . I have often expressed my sentiment, that every man, conducting himself as a good citizen, and being accountable to God alone for his religious opinions, ought to be protected in worshipping the Deity according to the dictates of his own conscience."[134]

To the Quakers: "The liberty enjoyed by the people of these States, of worshipping Almighty God agreeably to their consciences, is not only among the choicest of their *blessings*, but also of their *rights*. I assure you very explicitly, that in my opinion the conscientious scruples of all men should be treated with great delicacy and tenderness."[135]

To the Catholics: "May the members of your Society in America, animated alone by the pure spirit of Christianity . . . enjoy every temporal and spiritual felicity."[136]

To the Jews: "All possess alike liberty of conscience and immunities of citizenship. May the Children of the Stock of Abraham, who dwell in this land, continue to merit and enjoy the good will of the other Inhabitants. May the father of all mercies scatter light and not darkness in our paths."[137]

To a group of Presbyterian clergy concerned that the Constitution did not mention Christ by name: "The path of true piety is so plain as to require but little political direction."[138]

GOD AND GEORGE WASHINGTON

I believe that George Washington's words and actions throughout his career in military and political service are ample testimony to the vitality of his spiritual life. He was blessed with the skill and inner strength to see himself and America through decades of trial. As commander in chief he repeatedly called the army to prayer and worship. At the beginning of his presidency he publicly called the nation to God. At the end, in his Farewell Address, he reiterated the same theme.

Washington's continuity in command was miraculous in itself. He exposed himself to direct enemy fire often and was never even wounded. There were plots to supercede him through many dark periods of the war, when such plots might very well have been successful. He was often discouraged to the point of quitting. Through all, he persevered and continued in command. This continuity was in stark contrast to the frequent shifts in British leaders and was a key ingredient to his reputation and revered status, so vital to the new nation.

Some would say that America was "fortunate" to have George Washington as the key figure at the center of its founding. From my perspective, George Washington was another of God's many blessings on this nation. Without question, his military and political skills were essential to winning the war and to keeping the new and fractious republic together during its most critical years. A truly amazing combination of attributes made this possible. He was a man with the self-discipline and drive to achieve great goals. At the same time, he had remarkably little need for personal power and was able to step down when he had accomplished the task at hand. Washington himself frequently credited his abilities and successes to a higher power.

Washington's spiritual strength gave him an integrity and moral character that were fundamental to his success and inspirational to countless others. He continuously called his countrymen to a thankful and worshipful attitude toward God while exercising great care to separate political authority from matters of personal conscience. He tried to keep the nation focused on the source of its success but was content to leave the forms of worship to theologians, clergy, and individual citizens. It is truly difficult to imagine the shape that America might have taken without this man.

To conclude part two, the eloquent words of the historians Will and Ariel Durant are particularly appropriate: "So we end as we began, by perceiving that it was the philosophers and the theologians, not the warriors and diplomats, who were fighting the crucial battle of the eighteenth century."[139] So far we have seen the importance of philosophy and religion to the American Revolution. These endeavors of the mind were brought into reality through the monumental work of great, but practical men.

PART THREE
THE BATTLES

PART THREE
THE BATTLES

E VEN AS the American Revolution was evolving in the political and ideological areas, there was a war to be fought and won. Part three will focus on the battles that were key to this war.

George Washington continues as a significant figure in this story. As outlined in part two he was important to the political success of the new nation. Part three will show that he was even more vital to the success of the war effort. With few exceptions he was on the field of every important battle of the war. History judges him a great general in spite of many mistakes. Few have achieved as much under such difficult conditions. In the end, he gave the credit to the true central figure of this book, God himself: "The power and goodness of the Almighty were strongly manifested in the events of our late glorious revolution . . . In war he directed the sword and in peace he has ruled in our councils."[140]

Part three is not a complete history of the Revolutionary War as every battle is not addressed and some are mentioned only briefly. The battles presented are the most critical to the overall direction of the war. The details of these battles reveal how uncertain ultimate victory was at every stage of the war and provide even weightier evidence that much more than "good fortune" favored the young United States at the defining moments of its founding.

Chapter Five
Bunker Hill

On June 17, 1775, a group of hastily assembled and poorly trained New England militia units "lost" the Battle of Bunker Hill. As the sun set on the scene of this desperate daylong struggle, British forces held the high ground and their occupation of Boston was safe for a while longer. This seemed to be a dark day for those New England colonists committed to this fight with England. They had lost a battle and many good men without apparent gain. From the British perspective, however, this "victory" had cost more than they could afford to lose. The British army lost its aura of invincibility on that day. This perception had always been an important aspect of British power in the colonies. What should have been a rout had turned into a hard fought battle. An amazing outcome had taken place on this hill as a result of an amazing series of events. British and Americans fought bravely that day, but, as has so often been the case throughout the history of America, the outcome was in God's hand.

PRELIMINARIES

Early conflict between the American colonies and England seemed repeatedly to focus on one place, Boston. After the infamous "tea party" in 1773, Parliament passed a series of laws known as the Coercive Acts aimed straight at

Boston and the rest of Massachusetts. The Massachusetts colonial assembly was disbanded, and Lieutenant General Thomas Gage was sent as the new governor with power to appoint his own council. Gage also came to close the port of Boston, which he did on June 1, 1774. Life in the city came to a virtual standstill. Soon the once busy seaport was receiving only ships from England with supplies and troops to strengthen the British garrison. At the same time colonial militia units throughout New England and other colonies began forming, training, and stockpiling weapons and equipment. The colonials resolved to resist the apparent intention of the British to use military force to implement Parliament's edicts.

In September Gage sent a small expedition across the harbor to Charlestown to confiscate a stockpile of powder. This mission was carried out without incident although news of it spread like wildfire. By the next day, over four thousand armed colonials poured into Cambridge. In response to this uproar Gage ordered construction of defensive positions on Boston Neck, guarding the only land approach to the city. Tensions continued to mount as both sides prepared for the worst. In November Parliament authorized an additional six thousand troops for Gage's command. The colonial militia units stepped up their own preparations while carefully observing British activities in and around the city.

LEXINGTON AND CONCORD

During the predawn hours of April 19, 1775, a seven-hundred-man British expedition under Lieutenant Colonel Francis Smith was dispatched from Boston to confiscate reported stores of weapons and supplies and to arrest rebel leaders. Paul Revere and others made the famous ride by horseback that night to warn of

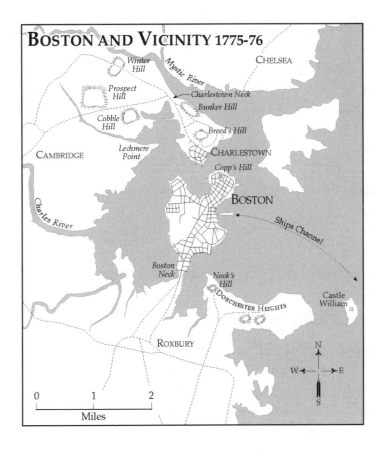

BOSTON AND VICINITY 1775-76

Winter Hill

Mystic River

CHELSEA

Prospect Hill

Charlestown Neck

Bunker Hill

Cobble Hill

Breed's Hill

Lechmere Point

CHARLESTOWN

CAMBRIDGE

Copp's Hill

Charles River

BOSTON

Ships Channel

Boston Neck

Nook's Hill

DORCHESTER HEIGHTS

Castle William

ROXBURY

N

W — E

S

0   1   2

Miles

the approaching redcoats. At Lexington the local militia company assembled early that morning to face the approaching British troops. During a tense confrontation, both forces exchanged fire, resulting in eight militiamen killed.

The British force continued on its route and reached Concord by mid-morning. Here the militia units withdrew ahead of the advancing redcoats, allowing the town to be occupied and searched. Not much was found as the locals had removed or hidden the military stores. The soldiers did discover three artillery pieces and quickly set fire to the wooden carriages. When smoke began to rise over the town, a nearby militia unit under the command of Colonel James Barrett advanced on Concord. A sharp engagement broke out at North Bridge where several colonial and British troops were killed.

At about noon, Lieutenant Colonel Smith reformed his men to begin the trek back to Boston. This march became a nightmare for the redcoats as they came under fire from local militia units all along the seventeen-mile march route. Both sides sustained casualties in fighting that lasted throughout the afternoon. By the time the British force got back to Boston it had lost over two hundred men. The conflict between the colonies and Britain had reached a new and alarming level.

THE SIEGE OF BOSTON

Within days of these events, thousands of New England militiamen assembled around Boston in Roxbury, Cambridge, and Chelsea. The fifteen Massachusetts regiments under the command of General Artemis Ward formed the largest contingent. By June the entire force swelled to about fifteen thousand men as troops continued to pour in from other areas of New England. Most agreed to place themselves loosely under General Ward's supervision. He had entrenchments and defensive works started around Cambridge and Roxbury. British forces continued to arrive by ship, including three new generals: Howe, Clinton, and Burgoyne.

At this time the second Continental Congress was meeting in Philadelphia in an air of crisis as tensions continued to mount throughout the colonies. A letter came from Massachusetts recommending that the New England militia units around Boston be used as a nucleus for a new Continental Army supported by all the colonies and controlled by Congress. Congress adopted this proposal and commissioned George Washington as the commander in chief. However, events around Boston did not wait for Washington to arrive.

Gage's naval commander, Admiral Samuel Graves, recommended at an early stage that the high ground around Boston be occupied for protection of his fleet. Gage had balked at this idea, choosing instead to pull all of his forces onto the Boston peninsula. However, by early June more troops were on hand, and the newly arrived generals were urging offensive action against the rebels. The generals agreed to a plan to attack Dorchester Heights on June 18, and to continue attacks on Roxbury and Charlestown. Information about these plans soon began filtering out to the colonial camps. General Ward and his advisors decided that their best defense in this situation was an offensive move of their own.

THE REBELS TAKE THE HILL

In the early evening of June 16, Col. William Prescott with his Massachusetts regiment of over eight hundred men moved quietly out of Cambridge and crossed Charlestown Neck. The highest point on the Charlestown peninsula was Bunker's Hill, and the entire peninsula was sometimes referred to by that name. Prescott's men climbed the hill, but then continued eastward to a lower elevation called Breed's Hill. From this point they could look across the Charles River to the Boston waterfront, only a half mile away. At around midnight the Massachusetts troops started work with picks and shovels to construct a redoubt on this key terrain.

The position covered an area less than fifty yards square, with projecting angles to allow interlocking fields of fire. Although never completely finished, the works would grow during the night and next day to a height of six feet above ground

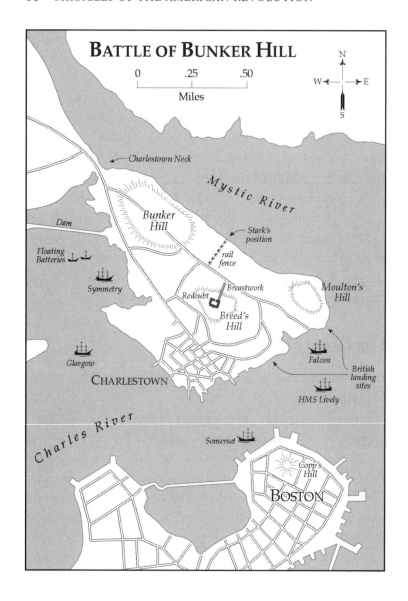

level with steps cut inside for firing positions. First light revealed to Prescott that the redoubt was exposed to the North, and his men extended a breastwork about one hundred yards in that direction. Later in the day, realizing that a large open area still lay between the breastwork and the bank of the Mystic River, Colonel Prescott detached Captain Thomas Knowlton with his two hundred Connecticut troops to fill that gap. Knowlton took up position behind a rail fence with a low stone footing, scattering his troops thinly to cover this large area.

Between two and three o'clock Colonel John Stark crossed Charlestown Neck with his First New Hampshire Regiment. This had become a dangerous maneuver, as British ships on the Charles River were able to sweep the narrow isthmus with cannon fire. Arriving on Breed's Hill, Stark assessed the situation quickly. He decided to place his men to bolster Knowlton's line along the rail fence.

As he positioned his men, Stark noticed that the extreme left flank of the line ended on the ground above the beach along the Mystic River. The beach itself was hidden from the higher ground and offered room for troops to pass even at high tide. He ordered two hundred of his men to build a stone wall across the beach to the water's edge. He placed a stake forty yards in front of the wall and ordered that no one open fire until the enemy reached the stake. Another officer of uncertain identity proclaimed the famous command, "Don't one of you fire until you see the white of their eyes!"

As time passed the day got hotter with each hour. It also became apparent that no one had planned for the resupply or relief of the troops that had been working all night. The men were exhausted, hungry and thirsty. They were also dangerously short of powder and shot. By midafternoon about

1,500 American militiamen were manning the line.[141] They could only wait and watch the British reaction to their efforts.

THE BRITISH WAKE UP

At first light on June 17, crewmen on HMS *Lively* observed the new activity on Breed's Hill from their anchorage in Boston harbor. The alarm sounded. The sailors warped the ship around on her anchor and brought her guns to bear on the rebel redoubt. Boston woke up that morning to the sound of *Lively*'s cannonade.

Soon after, General Gage called a council of war at his headquarters. General Clinton suggested a landing near Charlestown Neck to cut off and starve out this force on the peninsula. Gage dismissed this indirect approach quickly. He saw a long awaited opportunity to strike a decisive blow at the rebels by sending a direct assault on the redoubt. A quick rout of the rebels would demonstrate British determination and military superiority. Gage then placed General Howe in command of the attack.

As his troops and equipment were making preparations, Howe made his own reconnaissance by small boat. From the Mystic River he observed that the rebels were apparently not defending the northern side of Breed's Hill. From this observation he devised a two-pronged attack. He would send one force against the redoubt while another would attack north of the redoubt to cut off the rebel position and open it to destruction from the rear. Howe's attack would be supported by his own field artillery of brass six pounders, a battery of twenty-four pounders on Copp's Hill in Boston, and over two hundred naval guns. The naval weapons were deployed on the *Lively*, four other ships of the line, and two floating, shallow draft batteries.

A fleet of twenty-eight barges ferried the British attack force across the harbor. As the British buildup was in progress, Howe observed some of the rebel activity on the north slope of Breed's Hill. He did not change his plan of attack, but he did call for additional forces. He also asked Admiral Graves to move a ship or floating battery up the Mystic River to support his right flank. This request was denied. Admiral Graves would not send a ship into this area because it had not been charted and water depths were unknown.

By three o'clock Howe could wait no longer to start his attack. Deployed around him were three thousand regular British troops in line of battle.[142] General Pigot would lead the attack on the redoubt with about half of the force. Howe commanded the right wing, expecting to make the decisive breakthrough on that front. He assigned the beach attack to his light infantry companies, led by his own regiment, the Royal Welsh Fusiliers.[143]

The entire population of Boston had front-row seats for one of the most publicly viewed military engagements in history. The shore and ship batteries had been at work all day producing voluminous smoke and noise. They fired incendiary shells into Charlestown, engulfing the town in flames. The boatlift of troops across the harbor had been especially spectacular with an array of brightly colored uniforms and regimental colors flying. The main event was about to begin.

THE BATTLE OF BUNKER HILL

The British commanders did not have a high opinion of their opposition. They considered the hastily assembled farmers and tradesmen to be ill equipped, undisciplined, and even cowardly in light of their proclivity to hide behind things while fighting. On Breed's Hill the rebels were again hiding behind hastily prepared defensive positions. Even though Howe expected a

Battle of Bunker Hill (painting by John Trumbull—Yale University)

quick victory, he knew that caution was called for in this situation. Contrary to some accounts, he was not dumb. He designed his flank attack to bypass the strongest point and to quickly unravel the rebel positions from the flank and rear. Where he chose to attack frontally he intended to neutralize the enemy's advantage of prepared positions by using the shock effect of his field artillery.

Howe's artillery opened the battle with a flurry. Within a few minutes, however, the sound of the guns died. A runner soon reached General Howe to inform him that someone had brought the wrong sized shot across the harbor.[144] Instead of the proper six-pound cannonballs, twelve-pound ammunition was loaded in the side boxes. This news enraged Howe. He ordered that grape shot be fired, but this proved ineffective due to the range. He felt that he could not delay further, however, and ordered the advance without artillery support.

The Welsh Fusiliers were the first to reach the rebel line. They came in along the beach trotting seven abreast with weapons leveled expecting an ineffective first volley from any rebels on the beach and a quick bayonet fight, if any fight at all. Their advance continued without apparent opposition until they passed Stark's stake in the sand. Suddenly a firestorm erupted from the American line decimating rank after rank of Fusiliers. The attack dissolved as survivors pulled back in disorganized retreat.

This scene was replayed before the rail fence and the redoubt. Well-aimed fire and well-organized volleys decimated the British ranks. This devastating fire hit the officers especially hard as they tried valiantly and futilely to rally their men. Soon the dispirited and disorganized troops were back in the landing area where they had started. Howe and his officers regrouped for another effort. Giving up on the beach attack, Howe ordered a second assault on the high ground. This attack had the same result as the first. British dead and wounded littered the field.

The American defenders were having their own problems. Every man suffered from dehydration and each was near exhaustion after a night and day without relief or resupply. Ammunition was the critical factor. At this stage of the war the hastily assembled militia units had virtually no system of communications or logistics. General Ward dispatched orders to various units during the day to move to Breed's Hill. Many of these orders were misrouted or misunderstood. Colonel Prescott received very little support. Even so, he continued to courageously direct and encourage his men, preparing for yet another British attack.

To his credit as a leader and soldier, General Howe regrouped for a third attack even though many of his officers objected. Clinton arrived with fresh troops and the artillery was finally able to provide supporting fire with good effect, especially on the breastwork. At about five o'clock the infantry commenced their third assault focused primarily on the redoubt. An American volley again checked the advance, but this time the fire could not be

Colonel
John Stark
(painting
by Alonzo
Chappel—
National
Archives)

sustained. Continuous fighting had exhausted the ammunition
stocks. Colonel Prescott and his men had to give ground as the
redcoats came over the parapet. Fortunately, Knowlton and Stark
continued to hold the rail fence position from which they could
support the withdrawal of Prescott's men and prevent their being
cut off by the British advance. All along the line the Americans
fell back in good order. The redcoats crowded into the redoubt,
collapsed beside their weapons, and gave an exhausted victory
cheer. Boston and their reputation were saved.

GOD'S HAND AT BUNKER HILL

Bunker Hill should have closed the door on the American revolt. Up until this time there was no war. A clear-cut rout of the rebels on Breed's Hill would undoubtedly have prevented one. For months British reinforcements had poured into Boston, including the best of Britain's military leaders. By the time Prescott's men moved onto Breed's Hill, the British were ready for a fight. This was the time and perfect opportunity to teach a lesson to all the colonies. An undisputed victory would have given the clear message that insurrection was futile. The odds clearly favored this outcome. As events unfolded, however, God's hand moved to change the odds. He ensured that the rebellion would not be extinguished and would, instead, go on to a new level of intensity.

Although the Americans did not win this battle, they attained a distinct moral victory by their successive repulses of the attacking redcoats and orderly withdrawal from the hill. Fortunately Howe was not able to follow up on his gains. General Clinton urged continuing the attack on Cambridge, but Howe felt that this was impossible considering the condition of his command. The situation would have been vastly different if the British had routed the Americans early and easily. There were practically no defenses around Cambridge and the rebel headquarters. If the British had continued the attack on this area, the results would have been disastrous and could have collapsed the entire rebel line around Boston.

By modern standards casualties were light in this battle. There were 115 Americans killed and 305 wounded. The British lost 226 killed and 828 wounded.[145] However, British casualties represented over 40 percent of the attacking force, and at the time this was considered horrendous. Many units were decimated. One company of the Royal Welsh Fusiliers came out of the battle with only three men not killed or wounded.[146]

These losses affected General Howe deeply and seemed to make him excessively cautious after this point in the war. General Gage was recalled to England to face a reaction of shock and dismay. Instead of celebrating a victory, England had to face the fact there would be no quick end to conflict in the colonies.

At the time of Bunker Hill many in America considered the grievances with England to be a New England problem. Leaders of the resistance had no idea how far or in what direction events would lead. If no wider conflict had developed, they would have ended as little more than treasonous criminals. This would have been the situation if a rout of the New England militia units around Boston had occurred. Mass arrests of ringleaders and a complete extinguishing of the insurrection could well have followed. Instead, the courageous efforts of the colonial troops in this battle served to broaden the conflict and to bring a new level of unity to the colonies. Wide condemnation of the destruction of Charlestown helped serve the same purpose.

Paradoxically, the Americans almost learned the wrong lessons from this battle. Complete success in repelling the British attacks would have been convincing evidence of the effectiveness of the citizen soldier concept. If a spontaneous uprising of local militia could defeat British regular troops, what would be the need for a professional army? George Washington arrived in Cambridge a few days after the battle. What if Breed's Hill was occupied by New England militia units that had successfully beaten the redcoats while under the command of Artemis Ward, the new hero of New England? How would Washington have proceeded with his plans to organize, equip, and train a new Continental Army? It was as if God were orchestrating the precise degree of success at Bunker Hill to energize the young revolution without allowing any room for complacency to take hold.

Many circumstances contributed to the outcome of this battle. Throughout this intense action both British and American troops fought with conviction and courage. The leaders on both sides did their best to plan and direct events. They made some good decisions, and obviously made mistakes as well. Many historians seem to think that the British leadership was particularly inept. Some would also add that the British were extremely "unlucky." I believe that there was more at work here than incompetence or luck. God's purpose was accomplished at Bunker Hill when the British were denied a quick and convincing victory. God's providential hand can be seen in the many unusual circumstances that came together to produce that outcome.

The Wrong Objective. General Clinton's evaluation of the situation early on June 17 was militarily sound. His suggestion to attack and occupy key terrain on Charlestown Neck would have been the best tactical move. The American position on Breed's Hill was not a serious threat at that time as it lacked the weaponry to threaten Boston or Boston harbor. British forces on the Neck would have severed the rebel lines of supply and communications and would have forced the rebels to launch their own attack to eliminate this threat. It is highly unlikely that they would have organized such an attack. The rebel units on the peninsula would have eventually surrendered without a battle, and Charlestown would not have been destroyed. Pride and a low opinion of the Americans as soldiers dictated another course. British frustration over being on the defensive had built up for several months. Here finally was a chance for open combat and an opportunity to teach a lesson. The British took this rash approach in spite of the fact that their best military minds were on the scene and there was no need for haste. Selection of the wrong objective had severe consequences.

The Empty Beach. At some time during the afternoon of June 17, Colonel John Stark noticed the drop-off at the end of the rail fence. The empty beach below seemed to provide a possible way for enemy troops to move out of sight of the American lines. Although ignored by everyone else, the narrow beach along the Mystic River caught the attention of Stark. He immediately committed a force of two hundred men to the task of building a stone wall to the water's edge using material from the fields above. With the obvious threat to his front, he could well have decided just to keep the beach under observation or to place an outpost there. The British fusiliers running in massed column formation down the beach would have swept away anything other than a strong force behind good protection. Howe's main attack would have been a quick and devastating success.

No Naval Gunfire. Early in the afternoon General Howe observed some of the rebel activity on the north side of Bunker Hill where his main attack was to go. After ordering up reinforcements he asked Admiral Graves to send a warship or floating battery up the Mystic River to provide support from that direction. Graves turned him down. Even though British naval forces had been operating in and around Boston for over six months, no one had checked this particular area for navigability. This area was a short distance from the anchorage of Graves's own flagship. The most critical target of all lay there along the water's edge where Stark's men were constructing their stone wall. This area was untouched by Howe's cannon fire and was actually the best target of all for naval gunfire. Rebel activity on the beach could not have continued. Naval guns from this side could also have swept the rail fence, the least substantial of the rebel defenses. Admiral Graves's oversight in failing to reconnoiter the Mystic River was a critical factor in the course of the battle.

Meanwhile, the two hundred naval guns of Graves's fleet were blasting away on the other side of the peninsula at Charlestown and Bunker Hill. These guns produced voluminous quantities of smoke and noise without decisive effect. They destroyed Charlestown, but the cannonballs aimed at Bunker Hill either passed over the top of the redoubt or harmlessly impacted the hillside.

Wrong Cannonballs. As Howe prepared to order his infantry forward at about 3:30 in the afternoon, he did not know what lay ahead on the beach. He did know, however, that directly to his front was a hastily prepared rebel line along a rail fence. This area on the north slope of Breed's Hill was also immune to cannon fire from the Boston and ship batteries. Here was a mission for Howe's field artillery. The troops had laboriously brought these smaller, six pounders over the harbor by small boat and manhandled them up the hill. They had to breach fences and other obstructions to get the field pieces with their ammunition into position to fire on the rebels' fence line. This fire should have made the fence line untenable. When Howe learned that the wrong sized cannonballs were on hand it was too late to do anything about it. The infantry went into action without this critical support. The rail fence did not offer much protection to the Americans, but without cannon fire it was enough. Afterwards, a British supply officer was charged with negligence, when actually every gunner, ammunition handler, and officer should have shared the blame. It was amazing and miraculous that no one discovered this mistake before it was too late.

Chapter Six

Boston

As the sun rose over Boston harbor the colonial rifleman peered nervously across the wide expanse of water between his position and the Boston waterfront. The British garrison was beginning to stir. It was March 5, 1776. Since dusk the previous evening he and several thousand other American troops had labored to prepare artillery positions on the two prominent hills of Dorchester Heights. The view was breathtaking. The town of Boston and the British fleet at anchor were spread out below. All were now within range of the artillery pieces brought up during the night and fortified on the hills. Every man knew that the British could not tolerate this situation for long. A protracted winter of boredom was suddenly over. There was now the fear of imminent combat. After seven months of static siege around Boston, General George Washington had made his long awaited offensive move. There were many risks. The professional army of regular British troops concentrated in Boston was capable of striking in any direction. Bunker Hill was not a pleasant memory, and the sight of formations of redcoats continued to inspire fear and a sense of dread. The young rebellion seemed by many to be on borrowed time and was now at another critical moment. Washington could not afford a defeat, but knew that he had to take risks. He did not know of the many amazing events beyond his control that would unfold to affect the outcome of this pivotal confrontation.

WASHINGTON TAKES COMMAND

Three days after the battle of Bunker Hill, the president of the Continental Congress commissioned George Washington commander in chief of the newly formed Continental Army. Since his army was encamped around Boston, the forty-seven-year-old Washington left Philadelphia on horseback the next day. Before going twenty miles he was met by a courier with news of Bunker Hill. Early reports indicated that the battle was a major setback for the colonial cause.[147] He pressed ahead to make his own assessment, worried about what he would find in New England.

After meeting with the Massachusetts Assembly, Washington took formal command on July 3 at a brief ceremony in Cambridge. There was little pomp and circumstance. He knew that he had a difficult duty, and he faced it with a simple

Washington Takes Command (painting by M. A. Wageman—National Archives)

determination. He acknowledged his trust in Divine Providence to see him through successfully.[148]

Washington immediately inspected his men and their defensive positions. Both were lacking in most respects. His forces were stretched over a front of about ten miles from Chelsea to Roxbury in rough and somewhat haphazard entrenchments. The troops were mostly raw militia, unused to discipline or other military habits. There was no uniformity of appearance or procedures.

Instead of the twenty thousand men that he expected, Washington's first reports showed less than fourteen thousand, further depleted by sickness and furlough. Enlistments were due to expire for all of these troops by January 1 of the new year. By that time, he would have to recruit and organize a new Continental Army. This would not be easy in light of critical shortages in money, clothing, supplies, and shelter against a New England winter.

From Prospect Hill Washington could observe the new British outpost on Bunker Hill. There he saw professional entrenchments supported by navy ships strategically spotted in the harbor. At all points the veteran garrison of redcoats seemed to have the situation well in hand. Washington scarcely held superiority in numbers over his adversaries, and his troops were scattered over many miles, while the British were concentrated and capable of moving anywhere.

Washington soon began to make his presence felt. He insisted on improvements to all fortifications, doing his utmost to motivate all to new levels of effort in this labor-intensive activity. He ordered ten thousand hunting shirts to clothe the men and to achieve some military appearance. He stressed discipline and insisted on distinctions between officers and soldiers. Three divisions, or wings, were organized: the right on the Roxbury Heights under General Ward, the left on Winter and Prospect

Hills under Lee, and the center around Cambridge under command of General Putnam.

Throughout the fall and winter Washington continued his efforts to mold his army while facing the greatest difficulties. At one point an inventory revealed that the entire stock of gunpowder available would supply only nine rounds per man in the army. This fact circulated among the ranks, and a deserter eventually informed the British commanders in Boston.[149] They found this bit of information so unbelievable that it was discounted as a rebel trick.

The difficulty of Washington's situation is hard to comprehend. He had to reorganize and discipline the forces available, and, at the same time, attempt to recruit a new army largely from among the same troops. Clothing, equipment, and money were all in critically short supply. He could not complain of his plight publicly for fear of exposing his weakness. Few generals have had to deal with such dilemmas.

BRITISH ON THE DEFENSIVE

The one factor working in Washington's favor during this period came from the British failure to pursue the rebels as they withdrew from Bunker Hill. This decision by General Howe set the tone for months to follow. The British leaders, dispirited by their costly victory, seemed satisfied to defend Boston. Clinton alone agitated against this inaction and strongly advocated a move to take Dorchester Heights. An expedition was actually organized for this purpose a week after Bunker Hill but was postponed and then inexplicably abandoned. British staff officers did not believe the rebels could threaten from that quarter.[150]

Meanwhile, the British strengthened their other defenses. Howe did a thorough job of fortifying Bunker Hill, making this area impregnable to attack. He retained practically all of the forces used in the attack on the hill for its defense. Other units strengthened the Boston Neck defenses to the south. Naval forces manned ships and floating batteries in the Mystic River and harbor. Still, there continued to be no comparable concern over Dorchester Heights, directly overlooking the main ship channel and Boston waterfront. This did not change after October 10 when Howe became commander in chief and Gage returned to England.

FORT TICONDEROGA

In a separate campaign to the west, American forces led by Ethan Allen and Benedict Arnold captured Fort Ticonderoga on May 9, 1775. This key point joining Lake George and Lake Champlain controlled communications between New York and Canada. With the fort the Americans captured a large collection

The Guns from Ticonderoga (U.S. Army Signal Corps—National Archives)

of artillery pieces, gunpowder, and ammunition. In November 1775 General Washington conceived a project to transport these military stores to Boston.[151] He sent Henry Knox to New York to accomplish this mission. Arriving at Fort Ticonderoga on December 5, Knox selected forty-three cannon and sixteen mortars for the journey east. The cannon ranged in size from twelve to twenty-four pounders. Several of the mortars were the large thirteen-inch weapons averaging over a ton in weight.

The movement of these weapons to Boston is one of the great military epics of American history. Knox and his men had to move sixty tons of ordnance three hundred miles in winter.[152] The journey took them over Lake George, across the Hudson River four times, and through the Berkshire Mountains into Massachusetts. All arrived in late January 1776, giving Washington the capability of offensive action for the first time.

DORCHESTER HEIGHTS—THE PLAN

By early February General Washington seemed to see a glimmer of hope in his situation. About nine thousand men had signed one-year enlistments as Continental soldiers. Ten new regiments of New England militia arrived in camp, bringing his available forces to about seventeen thousand.[153] With the artillery pieces and ammunition delivered by Henry Knox, the time for action had arrived. The date was set for March 4, 1776.

Washington planned to move forces onto Dorchester Heights during the night and to prepare defensive positions as rapidly as possible. He expected this move to force Howe's hand. The British would either have to come out of Boston to attack the heights, or else they would have to evacuate the city.

Expecting an attack, Washington made thorough preparations. His forces would have to do their work during one night in anticipation of a probable assault the next day. Ground frozen to a depth of eighteen inches made a difficult task almost impossible.[154] Colonel Rufus Putnam of Massachusetts devised the solution to this problem.[155] He planned to place bundles of sticks, or fascines, in wooden frames on top of the ground. His men prepared these in large quantities ahead of time to add mass to fortifications that were extremely difficult to dig.

Another measure taken by Washington was a request to the Massachusetts legislature to assemble militia units from surrounding towns. The locals honored this request and provided valuable reinforcements to meet the expected British counterattack.[156]

An artillery bombardment of Boston was integral to Washington's plan. His newly installed batteries at Lechmere Point, Cobble Hill, and Roxbury opened fire during the evening of March 2.[157] Although the bombardment did little damage, the British were shocked by the large caliber weapons used against them for the first time. The bombardment continued the next night and became even heavier during the night of the 4th when the actual move to the heights took place. In unwitting cooperation, the British batteries in Boston responded in kind, adding to the noise and smoke and further masking any indication of rebel troop activity.

HEIGHTS TAKEN

At about 7:00 p.m. on March 4, 1776, Washington's forces began to move. A covering party of about eight hundred men reached the peninsula, divided, and occupied the areas closest to Boston and Castle William. Their mission was to provide local security and to make little noise. Troops stacked hay beside the road to shield movement from view. About 1,200 men under

General Thomas moved directly to the two highest points on the peninsula. Three hundred oxcarts loaded with fascines and supplies supported the operation.[158] These carts made repeated trips during the night. Officers laid out the defensive works according to plan, and the fascines were put into place. Some worked diligently with pick and shovel to dig down as much as possible and to add soil to the works.

Conditions during the night were perfect for the Americans. Temperatures were mild. On the hills, moonlight shown brightly. At the lower elevations and across the harbor, a smoky haze restricted visibility from the town and anchorages. The frozen ground made entrenching difficult but greatly expedited the movement of men and materiel by cart. Even the wind cooperated, coming from the southwest, carrying sound away from the town. The wind also blew smoke from the Roxbury batteries across the harbor, contributing to the haze.

Planning and preparation paid off as work progressed rapidly through the night. By 10:00 p.m. construction of the two main fortifications was advanced to the point where they could be defended against small arms and grapeshot.[159] Improvements continued. At around 3:00 a.m. fresh troops relieved the initial force on the heights. These men continued to work on the fortifications and prepared to defend them against the expected British attack.

THE BRITISH WAKE UP (AGAIN)

It was an eerie replay of June 17 the year before. As the sun came up on March 5, 1776, surprise seemed to be complete within the British garrison. All were amazed at the apparent extent of rebel activity on the hills to the south. Howe is reported to have stated, "The rebels have done more in one night than my whole army would have done in months."[160] British reports estimated that as many as twenty thousand Americans were employed in the occupation and fortification of the new positions.[161] British batteries on shore and ship attempted to react to this new threat, but were unable to elevate guns sufficiently for effective fire.

Washington's estimate of the situation proved correct. Howe could not ignore this new development. The British commander's senior admiral soon informed him that it would be impossible to keep ships in the harbor under these conditions.[162] Although the rebels were not yet on Nook's Hill, this seemed a likely next move. If this were to occur, British defensive works on Boston Neck would actually be vulnerable to fire from the rear. Howe resolved to clear Dorchester Heights of this threat.

BRITISH "ATTACK"

Howe gave Brigadier General Jones the mission of driving the Americans off the hill with an assigned force of 2,200 men. By noon on the 5th the Boston waterfront was a beehive of activity. Men and equipment assembled and began moving by small boat to waiting transport vessels. Once again, the local populace began to gather at likely vantage points to view another epic clash. Five regiments embarked, and by early evening two more were waiting for boats.

The assault force moved across the harbor toward Castle William. The first phase of the attack was to be a landing on the point of Dorchester peninsula opposite the castle. From the landing area they would attack the easternmost rebel fort first. This would mask the fires from the other rebel fort, enabling each to be defeated separately. The landing required that troops and equipment be put into small boats for the movement to shore. Although this operation was to take place in generally sheltered waters, much depended on reasonable conditions of tide, wind, and surf.

At this point, the weather took control of events. In the early evening a sudden storm came up, described by one local observer at the time as a "hurrycane."[163] The storm was of an intensity that few had seen.[164] The surf conditions on the Dorchester beaches made landing small boats out of the question. The storm scattered even the transport ships, driving three aground on Governor's Island. The storm continued through the night, and the next morning torrential rains persisted.

On the morning of March 6, Howe assembled his subordinates. He feared that the rebels had so strengthened their positions over the previous day that an attack was then too dangerous. Since the opportunity had passed for offensive action, he ordered his forces back into garrison. There would be no British attack on Dorchester Heights.

THE LIBERATION OF BOSTON

Instead of an attack, Howe ordered an evacuation. This was the outcome that Washington had hoped would occur. Howe's order initiated a period of intense activity among his forces. Every person and item of equipment leaving Boston had to go on available shipping. Due to limitations of space, considerable stores, heavy weapons, and horses were abandoned. The departing troops left about two hundred fifty artillery pieces behind after attempting to destroy them. Later the Americans succeeded in making many of these weapons serviceable.

This activity was not alarming to the soldiers. However, the loyalist inhabitants of Boston, who had placed themselves under the king's protection, were in a state of shock.[165] These unfortunates feared a future under the conquering rebels and suddenly faced the end of their way of life. Over a thousand chose to gather a few personal belongings and scramble for berths on available ships. Most who left never returned.

General Howe managed to communicate to Washington that his troops would not destroy Boston if the Americans would not contest his evacuation. In spite of Howe's orders, however, there was widespread looting on the part of his own soldiers. There was also a certain amount of "official" looting to remove clothing and stores that might be of use to the rebels. This activity continued for several days.

As a final encouragement to the British evacuation, Washington fortified Nook's Hill during the night of March 16. From this point the American forces were able to directly threaten the British defenses on Boston Neck and the Boston waterfront. By ten o'clock the next day, St. Patrick's Day, the British fleet was under sail. The eleven-month siege was over.

Continental Congress Votes for Independence (painting by Robert Pine and Edward Savage—National Archives)

Washington had no time to celebrate his victory. All signs seemed to indicate that Howe would proceed to New York with his forces. In anticipation of this, Washington began to move his own troops in that direction. Initially, the British fleet sailed to Halifax. There the civilians debarked, and preparations began for the expected campaign in New York.

GOD'S HAND AT DORCHESTER HEIGHTS

Since no battle took place on Dorchester Heights, untold bloodshed was avoided. The battle would have been costly for both sides, even though this time the advantage was with the Americans. They had artillery and carefully hoarded stocks of powder. Fresh troops came up during the night to do the fighting. Unlike Bunker Hill, the Americans were ready for this fight.

The British had incentives of their own to fight for this terrain. The Americans were threatening their hold on Boston and professional reputations were at stake. Formations of British redcoats still possessed that aura of invincibility for which they were famous. The results of a determined assault on the easternmost redoubt are difficult to estimate. The outcome was not a sure thing. The only sure thing would have been high casualties. Many thanked God that this did not occur.

Howe had other options available to respond to the situation facing him on March 5, 1776. Instead of a difficult amphibious operation across the harbor, he could have attacked by land along Boston Neck, directly threatening Roxbury and cutting off Washington's forces on Dorchester. Such an attack would have jeopardized the rest of the thinly held American lines around Boston. Whether Howe did not see such an option or whether he simply did not have the nerve to implement it is an interesting point of speculation. The fact is, he did have options, and the outcome of this confrontation was never a sure thing.

Howe's decision to give up the contest may have saved him some degree of embarrassment. On the other hand, it may have saved Washington from a catastrophe. This was another crucial moment in the revolution when a defeat would have been disastrous to the American cause. Instead, with God's help and Howe's default, Washington achieved a great victory.

Political developments within the Continental Congress reveal the full significance of these events in Boston. Representatives from the colonies continued the protracted and frustrating dispute with King George and Parliament. By early 1776 the situation looked more grim than ever. The king had rejected the so-called Olive Branch Petition, approved by Congress in 1775, and had declared the colonies to be in a state of rebellion. British reinforcements continued to arrive in Boston. There seemed to be a tenuous military stalemate in Massachusetts and growing problems keeping a colonial army in the field.

There was also a stalemate within Congress between radical and conservative factions. The radical agenda seemed to be moving toward independence from England and formation of a new nation. The conservatives were committed to a redress of grievances and a return to normal times. They feared a war and probable ruin and continued hoping for reconciliation. This approach had prevailed so far during Congress's deliberations, even to the point where delegates from six colonies were under specific instructions to vote against independence.

This picture changed on March 23 when word arrived from Massachusetts that the army had forced the British to abandon Boston. Celebrations broke out in Philadelphia. The tone of the debate in Congress changed. In April the delegates from South

Carolina, Georgia, and North Carolina received instructions permitting a vote for independence.

The momentum of events gathered from this point. In early May, Congress passed a resolution that individual colonies assume all powers of government. On June 7, 1776, Richard Henry Lee from Virginia rose before Congress to move "That these United Colonies are, and of a right ought to be, free and independent states." Lee's motion was taken up on July 1 and the issue addressed that Adams called "the greatest question ever debated in America and as great as ever was debated among men."[166] On the next day twelve colonies voted in favor of the resolution, with only New York abstaining.

On July 4 Congress formally ratified the Declaration of Independence, and each of the fifty-six delegates individually signed the document.

During this critical period the delegates themselves frequently turned to God. John Adams stated, "It is the will of heaven that the two countries should be sundered forever," placing his fate in an overruling Providence.[167] The United States of America would be under the authority and protection of God and based on God-given rights. Samuel Adams rose in the assembly to state, "We have this day restored the Sovereign, to Whom alone men ought to be obedient."[168]

Washington's success at Boston had many ramifications. Boston was liberated. The Continental Army did not suffer disastrous casualties or defeat. The fire of rebellion survived, just as it had at Bunker Hill. This time, however, the political ramifications were dramatic. As a direct result of this military success, the Continental Congress moved to the irreversible step of independence. The Founding Fathers, praying for God's protection, committed themselves to a course leading either to a new nation or disaster.

Instead of a victory celebration, Washington asked for a church service and thanksgiving. With his officers he listened to a sermon by Dr. Elliot, a Boston clergyman. Elliot preached on a biblical passage from Isaiah: "Your eyes will see Jerusalem, a peaceful abode, a tent that will not be moved." The passage concludes with the assertion: "The Lord is our King; it is he who will save us."[169] Clearly George Washington himself firmly believed those words. He knew that God had saved the army at Boston and brought a great victory. He knew better than anyone else every detail of the campaign that pointed to the hand of Providence.

Washington's Plight Ignored. Through the long winter of 1775–76 Washington struggled to keep his army from dissolving. The pitiful supply of gunpowder at one point rendered him almost without military capability. When this information made its way to the British headquarters, General Howe chose not to believe it and continued to hold his forces in Boston. He mounted no operations or even significant probes of the rebel lines. Howe gave Washington the gift of precious time to recruit and supply his struggling army.

Dorchester Heights Ignored. In June 1775 the Americans fought a battle over Bunker Hill to head off British plans to occupy Dorchester Heights. This key terrain dominated the Boston waterfront and shipping channels. At least one British general kept this objective in mind. General Howe, however, chose to ignore these heights for over seven months and to overlook advice to take them.

> Howe had concluded that, without heavy artillery, the rebels could pose no threat from this quarter. He should have been alert to any change in this situation. Somehow no information reached him about the movement of weapons from Fort

Ticonderoga. However, he should have figured out something for himself on March 2. On that evening the Americans opened fire with their newly acquired big guns. The warning was clear for two days that a new threat existed. Still, no alarm bells sounded within the British high command in Boston.

A Warning Ignored. In Boston a British officer received a report at about 10:00 p.m. on the night of March 4, that "the rebels were at work on Dorchester Heights."[170] Brigadier General Francis Smith had been the leader of the Lexington/Concord expedition almost one year before. He was not destined to be famous for his energy or initiative. He received the report and did nothing with it. He took no action to confirm the information. No artillery fire was directed that night toward Dorchester. No one assembled troops or made plans. Smith allowed dawn to come and Howe to discover for himself what had happened during the night. Those lost hours proved fatal to the British occupation of Boston.

Perfect Weather. Weather conditions could not have been better for the Americans on the night of March 4. Mild temperatures and a clear night on the heights facilitated the movement onto the hills and construction of fortifications. The frozen ground was first considered a major hindrance to the operation. However, when this problem was solved, the hard ground proved a blessing to the movement of men and oxen over difficult terrain. Mud would have made it impossible to get heavy artillery into position. Amazingly, while visibility was perfect on the heights, smoke, and haze were extensive at ground level. A favorable wind caused the smoke to screen American movements and to carry noise away from Boston.

Perfect Storm. What Timothy Newell described as a "hurry-cane" came at the exact moment to benefit the American cause. The storm made Howe's attack impossible for a fateful day. The Americans used the time to decisive advantage, continuing all possible efforts to strengthen their fortifications. The critical moment passed. Howe reached the conclusion that it was then too late to take any action against Washington's forces, and he instead abandoned Boston. The cancellation of Howe's attack saved untold bloodshed. It also may have saved Washington's army and the Revolution.

CHAPTER SEVEN
LONG ISLAND

The young soldier could not believe his eyes. Only minutes before he could see nothing unusual as he gazed over the broad reaches of New York Bay. Now, a virtual forest of ships' masts filled his view. Private Daniel McCurtin of the Maryland Rifles recorded in his diary, "I declare, at my noticing this, that I could not believe my eyes . . . In about ten minutes the whole bay was full of shipping as ever it could be . . . I thought all London was afloat." McCurtin was one of many Continental soldiers preparing to defend New York during the summer of 1776. They expected a British offensive. However, what was unfolding was far beyond anyone's expectations. No one had seen an array of military force of this magnitude.

AS THE BRITISH sailed from Boston in March 1776, the attention of all turned to New York City, the strategic center of the colonies. New York was the vital link between New England and the southern colonies. Transportation, communications, and commerce between North and South came together at this point. Here also, the Hudson River entered the Atlantic, providing the most direct route to and from Canada. New York was second only to Philadelphia in size and had a seaport second to none. It also happened to have a very large population loyal to the crown.

THE AMERICANS PREPARE

George Washington arrived in New York on April 13 to take charge of defensive preparations that were already under way. Congress was insistent the city be held. Washington believed this was possible, although he faced the dilemma of any commander with an opponent controlling the sea. The British could strike anywhere, and he had to allocate forces to cover each possibility.

Washington's nine-thousand-man army became a large construction gang, building forts, digging trenches, and erecting obstacles. They constructed gun batteries on Manhattan, the New Jersey shore, and Long Island to control the waterways and to protect the city. Trench networks were excavated to defend against ground attack. Two large forts, named Washington and Lee, were constructed upriver at a point where ships could be sunk across the river as a barricade.

Considering recent events in Boston, the area known as Brooklyn Heights took on special significance. These heights lay about a mile east of the Manhattan waterfront across the East River, commanding the river and port facility. New York would be untenable if the enemy held this area. The defense of Brooklyn Heights would require a sizable force and a dangerous division of Washington's forces. Even so, he could not avoid it.

During the summer of 1776 new units continued to report for duty in New York, until Washington's effective strength approached nineteen thousand men.[171] These were divided among the defensive works in progress. Most were new recruits with few skills and little discipline and totally unprepared for combat. Even so, morale was high among the Americans.

The Continental Congress issued the Declaration of Independence on July 4, clarifying the nature of the cause and motivating every man with an even stronger sense of purpose.

Considering recent events at Bunker Hill and Dorchester Heights, the colonial troops had reason to expect success. Their preparations and obvious determination to fight might deter the British from even attempting an invasion. If an attack did come, they would be fighting from prepared positions like those so successfully employed around Boston. Unfortunately, this was to prove wishful thinking. There was no way for them to know what was coming.

THE BRITISH ARRIVE

On June 25, 1776, three British warships appeared in lower New York Bay. Over a hundred more vessels joined these within a few days. General William Howe had arrived from Halifax with his army, reorganized and refitted since leaving Boston. Troops began disembarking on Staten Island without opposition. By mid-August additional forces arriving straight from Great Britain brought the ship total to over four hundred and troop strength to thirty-two thousand. These were fully equipped, trained, and disciplined soldiers. About one-fourth were German mercenaries, collectively referred to as "Hessians."[172]

The British king and Parliament had decided that they needed to inflict a devastating blow to regain control of the colonies quickly and completely. To accomplish this they amassed the largest military force ever before deployed overseas by Britain in August 1776.

The Americans could only wait to see where the blow would fall. General Washington told his men, "The fate of unborn millions will now depend, under God, on the courage and conduct of this army. Let us, therefore, rely upon the goodness of the cause and the aid of the Supreme Being, in whose hands victory is, to animate and encourage us to great and noble actions."[173]

BATTLE OF LONG ISLAND

- - - American forward
        positions
⊔——⊡ American main line
◄- - - - British attacks

0   1   2   3
Miles

FORT LEE

FORT WASHINGTON

N
W   E
S

Hudson River

NEW JERSEY

Long Island Sound

Hoboken

NEW YORK

East River

Long Island

Wallabout Bay

Ferry
BROOKLYN

Bushwick

Governor's Island

New York Bay

Gowanus Bay

(Howe)   Jamaica Pass

Bedford

Flatbush Pass

Flatbush

Narrows

New Utrecht

(Howe)

Flatlands

Staten Island

Gravesend

Gravesend Bay

THE BRITISH MOVE

On August 22, 1776, General Howe was finally ready to commence operations. With a fleet of seventy-five flatboats and other craft he began transporting his army across the Narrows to Gravesend Bay on Long Island.[174] Howe took several days to deliberately build up his forces, stock supplies, and prepare for operations to come.

During the initial British buildup on Long Island, Washington believed that a feint was in progress to divert his attention from Manhattan. Therefore, at first he was reluctant to send reinforcements. He was also having command problems on Long Island. General Greene, the officer who knew the most about the terrain and defenses there, became sick and unfit for duty. General John Sullivan had been in command for several days but was superceded on August 24 by General Israel Putnam. By August 26 there were about seven thousand colonial defenders on Long Island.[175] Although they represented a sizable portion of Washington's army, they were hardly adequate to hold off the forces gathering against them.

These Americans on Long Island were organized into two defensive lines. The main line with about four thousand men lay across Brooklyn Heights, stretching almost one mile between Wallabout Bay and Gowanus Bay. Five strong points or forts with interconnecting trench works anchored this line. Stakes and felled trees ahead of the line provided obstacles to enemy movement. This was a strong, though uncompleted, position.

Between the main line and British encampments on the plains, a series of low hills ran across the island at an oblique angle. These hills were heavily wooded and easily passable only on the existing roads going up through the passes. The Americans established a forward line to defend the three most likely passes giving access to Brooklyn Heights. About 2,800 men manned this line in isolated locations with practically no way to coordinate between themselves.[176] These positions were far more than a screen as they were designed for stubborn defense. However, if the British penetrated or bypassed any one, all the others would be in danger of being cut off. Unfortunately, such coordination would prove to be impossible.

THE BATTLE OF LONG ISLAND

With a steady flow of information on the rebel defenses coming in from Tory sympathizers, General Howe carefully made his plans.[177] On August 26 he positioned his forces for three attacks. One body was to move along the west bank road near the Narrows. One was to attack the Flatbush Pass. Both of these elements were to make a show of force the next morning in front of the rebel positions until a signal was given for the all-out assault. The third force would be the main attack, led by Howe himself. This force would sweep around the left flank of the rebel forward line.

After nightfall on August 26, Howe directed his units on a nine-mile march through Jamaica Pass. Using local guides, he planned to exploit a glaring weakness in his enemy's defense. Inconceivably, the Americans' left flank was unguarded and "in the air." The only measure taken by the Americans to guard this flank was a party of five mounted officers dispatched that same night to provide early warning of any unexpected activity along the Jamaica Road. Again, inconceivably, all five of these officers were captured together and failed totally in their mission.

Action started early on August 27 along the American forward line as the British and Hessian diversionary attacks began. Sharp engagements were fought at isolated locations as the defenders held their ground. These actions served their purpose perfectly. The attention of the Americans remained focused on these attacks at the passes that they were expecting.

By nine in the morning the lead elements of Howe's flanking force reached Bedford without opposition or even detection. At that point they were closer to the main defensive position on Brooklyn Heights than were most of the American forward positions. Two cannon shots were fired as the signal for the general assault by all British units.[178]

Chaos ensued within the American ranks as men in the forward positions found themselves completely surprised and fighting in two directions. British forces surrounded and captured entire units and disbursed others as men fled through the woods individually and in small groups.

By 2:00 p.m. the forward defensive line had ceased to exist. An orderly defense had turned into a rout. William Howe had learned his lesson well at Bunker Hill. He had cleverly and

Battle of Long Island (U.S. Army Signal Corps—National Archives)

deliberately avoided a frontal assault on prepared positions. He achieved complete surprise and was able to watch his foe crumble on all fronts. American losses, including casualties and captured, totaled over one thousand men. Howe lost fewer than four hundred.[179] A victory such as this at Bunker Hill would undoubtedly have brought a quick end to the Revolution.

THE HALT

The dispirited remnants of American units flooded into the Brooklyn Heights positions, closely pursued by advancing British and Hessian formations flushed with success. Heavy firing broke out all along the line. The disorganized Americans could only wait apprehensively for the final assault. Howe's subordinate commanders requested and then pleaded for permission to deliver the final blow.[180] Howe would not give it. He instead ordered a halt and a consolidation of his forces.

Historians have criticized Howe for his decision to stop the attack on Long Island on August 27, 1776. If he had gone on and successfully taken Brooklyn Heights, he would have destroyed or captured major elements of the American army and most of its military leaders, including George Washington himself.

Howe may have been overcautious on this occasion and too conscious of his experience at Bunker Hill. In this situation, however, he felt that time was on his side. He thought that he had time to consolidate his forces and to construct trench lines closer to the American positions. He also felt that he could wait for his brother, Admiral Dick Howe, to maneuver ships up the East River to totally cut off the American defenders on Long Island.

There was every reason to expect that the British fleet would play a decisive role in the battle. Earlier, on July 12, the British ships *Phoenix* and *Rose* had successfully voyaged up the Hudson River past every American battery and sunken obstacle. The American guns were ineffective and too few to do the job. A squadron of British warships was ready on August 27 to support the ground attack, but unfavorable winds hampered their efforts during the day.[181] Howe expected a decisive naval penetration into the East River at any time.

THE WEATHER

Prevailing winds along the New York coast in August are normally from the southeast.[182] This would have been ideal for British naval operations in this action. The northeasterly winds of August 27 turned instead into a powerful storm from the same direction with high winds and heavy rains throughout August 28 and 29.[183] These conditions brought untold misery to the Americans huddled in trenches filled with water and now burdened with totally soaked weapons and equipment.

At this point, however, the weather was more than uncomfortable to the British. It completely frustrated Admiral Howe's naval squadron in moving upriver during both of these days. Only during the night of the 29th did the winds slack off, enabling preparations for action the next day.[184] Meanwhile, General Howe's trench digging effort toward the American lines proceeded slowly, also severely hampered by the miserable weather.

RETREAT

After the disaster on August 27, Washington remained on Long Island and reinforced his army there until he had about nine thousand troops in the Brooklyn defenses. On August 29 he finally began to realistically assess the danger of his situation.

He was keenly aware of the enemy's trench-building efforts. If these proceeded much closer to his lines, he would have to order men out of their defensive positions to deal with the threat. His troops would then be the ones in the open trying to dislodge others from covered positions.

He was also aware of the naval threat and the earlier British success on July 12 in penetrating his river defenses. He knew that the river obstacles between Governors Island and Manhattan were equally inadequate and that no obstacles were in place between Governors Island and Brooklyn.[185] The British could isolate him from Manhattan at any time. He could not afford to continue risking half his army. He decided that the time had come to cut his losses.

Once he made the decision to retreat, Washington proceeded masterfully. He communicated his intentions to few others. He orchestrated the retreat to appear even to his own men as a relief of lines by fresh units from Manhattan. He actually issued orders to this effect. On this occasion George Washington did manage to tell a lie.

The American forces gathered boats all day on August 29. The 14th and 27th Massachusetts Regiments, led by John Glover and Israel Hutchinson, were called off the lines to man the boats. Seamen and fishermen filled the ranks of these units, and they were perfectly suited to this mission. A two-mile round-trip faced these men. They would have to make it time and again at night under harsh conditions of wind and rain.

The greenest troops moved first to the landing for evacuation. The best units gradually spread across the line to keep up the sounds and appearance of a normal defensive position. As each hour went by, these men faced increasing danger that the enemy would discover the evacuation. There was no possibility that they could hold off an attack or even a serious probe.

Any British unit advancing through the depleted American line would have caused utter havoc to the already confused movement of men and equipment to the waterfront.

Early in the evening it appeared to the officer in charge of the embarkation at the Brooklyn ferry that it would be impossible to get the job done that night due to adverse conditions of wind and tide. He sent an aide to give this information to General Washington, but the aide could not locate the general in the darkness and confusion.[186] The evacuation continued.

At around eleven that evening the weather again seemed to bless the Americans. The wind died down, easing the problem of moving full boats across the river. As the water calmed, the seamen loaded the boats to within inches of the gunnels. Also, for the first time, they could use all of the sailboats, enabling a great increase in the rate of progress.[187] It would still be a close race with daylight and discovery by the British.

At about 2:00 a.m. an almost fatal blunder occurred. One of Washington's aides erroneously ordered the final covering party, commanded by General Thomas Mifflin, off the lines. Before they could be turned around, almost an hour of deadly silence elapsed along the American line. The covering force would remain in position until about 6:00 a.m. the next morning, keeping up the campfires and intermittent noises of soldiers in camp.[188]

During the night danger arose from still another quarter. Mrs. John Repelye lived near the Brooklyn ferry landing. The Americans suspected that she and her husband were loyalists and had even detained her husband. That night, seeing a retreat in progress, she dispatched her Negro servant to inform the British commander or any officer that he could find. After carefully working his way past the American lines, the Negro was apprehended by a Hessian patrol. The Hessians could not understand English or any of the black man's message. They kept him under guard until the next morning when, too late, he finally found a British officer to receive his report.[189]

With the approaching dawn on August 30 the Americans left on Long Island were very apprehensive. Even before first light, suspicious British and Hessian pickets were probing the unnaturally quiet lines. They would discover the retreat at any moment, making further withdrawal too dangerous to contemplate. General Washington himself waited at the ferry landing determined to be the last off the island.

Just before dawn, the weather intervened once again on behalf of the Americans. A thick and unexpected fog rose off the river. It was described by Major Benjamin Tallmadge who found himself in it: "As the dawn of the next day approached, those of us who remained in the trenches became very anxious for our own safety, and when the dawn appeared there were several regiments still on duty. At this time a very dense fog began to rise, and it seemed to settle in a peculiar manner over both encampments. I recollect this peculiar providential occurrence perfectly well; and so very dense was the atmosphere that I could scarcely discern a man at six yards distance."[190] William Gordon described the same scene, in his own picturesque way referring to it as "that *heavenly messenger*, the fog." A citizen of New York informed Gordon that such a fog in that season had not been known for twenty to thirty years.[191]

Under cover of the fog, the remainder of Washington's army and Washington himself embarked in small boats and cleared the Brooklyn shoreline. The advancing British troops fired at the last boats and captured one of them with four men.[192] The fog and calm conditions also prevented any movement by British ships that morning to disrupt the final stages of the retreat. Major Tallmadge concluded, "The providential appearance of the fog saved a part of our army from being captured, and certainly myself among others who formed the rear guard."

By mid-morning on August 30, 1776, the defenders of Long Island scattered throughout Manhattan in a state of total exhaustion. The days of misery in knee-deep water, soaking rain, and constant anxiety had taken their toll. Morale was about as low as it could go in an army that had been defeated and forced to retreat under cover of darkness. The only emotion in evidence was relief. For now they were at least safe.

AFTERMATH

Morale plummeted throughout the colonies with news of Long Island. Anxiety and fear spread with the realization that the victorious British and Hessian forces seemed unstoppable. New recruits and supplies became even more difficult to obtain. These events encouraged and emboldened loyalists everywhere in their support of the advancing forces of the Crown. Silas Deane wrote to Congress from Paris, "The want of instructions or intelligence or remittances, with the late check on Long Island, has sunk our credit to nothing."[193]

The report of General Howe's Long Island victory reached England on October 10, 1776. This news touched off celebrations in the streets, with bells ringing and cannon firing. British stocks soared on the Amsterdam exchange.[194] The king conferred the Order of the Bath on General Howe, now hailed as the man who had "won" the war.

American gloom and British euphoria both went too far. Long Island was indeed a disaster for the Americans. However, it was not the total disaster that would have ended the war. It was not the total disaster that would have resulted from the destruction of the Continental Army or the capture of George Washington.

GOD'S PROVIDENCE AT LONG ISLAND

The battle of Long Island was an unexpected disaster for the colonies. Only six months before, the British had sailed away from Boston, and less than two months had elapsed since an optimistic Congress had defiantly proclaimed independence. Many colonists hoped that the British might call off further military action. They had surrendered Boston without a fight, and had given up a naval advance on Charleston in June. Talks were ongoing in Britain about forming a peace commission to America.[195] The defensive works around New York seemed formidable. There were hopes that these displays of colonial determination might be enough. These hopes evaporated on Long Island.

There had been no reckoning the determination of the British king and Parliament to smash the revolt. The king appointed Lord George Germain, an advocate of "bringing the rebels to their knees," to the post of secretary for the colonies.[196] Although many in Parliament were sympathetic to colonial interests, the king and his majority were able to consistently override opposition to the strongest measures.[197] They amassed a fleet and army without regard to cost, with the overwhelming power to end the conflict in America with one decisive stroke.

At this point in history God seemed to be saying to the struggling revolutionaries in America that freedom was not going to come easily or without a price. Like the Egyptians, in the biblical book of Exodus, the British were also not going to just let "their" colonies walk away. If for some reason they had, there is a strong possibility that thirteen new and independent nations would have been the result. This was not God's plan for America. There would be a struggle, and, for this struggle to be won, there would have to be unity and commitment to a common cause. God would mold the Americans together and forge a new nation through these hardships.

Washington and his generals made many mistakes on Long Island. Many shared the blame for the disastrous rout of August 27. Washington himself was slow to grasp the danger of his situation and waited too long to abandon Brooklyn. His inexperience showed at every turn. With God's help, however, he was able to learn on the job and adapt to the reality of circumstances around him. He was a proud man, but he learned to listen to others and to accept good advice. Under the pressure of a determined enemy, miserable weather conditions, and personal exhaustion, he listened to his subordinates and to God. He made the right decision to save his army.

Once he made the decision, Washington proceeded to plan and conduct one of the most difficult and dangerous operations possible in combat: a retreat across a major natural obstacle while still engaged with the enemy. Thanks to Washington's generalship and to God's providential hand, this operation succeeded. The army was saved, and a small spark of hope was provided to a demoralized population.

Howe's Halt. If General Howe had assaulted Washington's main defensive line on Brooklyn Heights on August 27, there would have been a bloody battle, and he would undoubtedly have paid a heavy price. The prize would have been the rebel army and George Washington himself. This would have ended the war that day. Few commanders have such opportunities, and Howe's subordinates sensed it. I believe that God used Howe's own cautious nature to blind him to the potential of this crucial moment. Howe focused on his experience at Bunker Hill and remembered his losses storming the rebels' prepared defenses. He overlooked the fact that a time comes in war for decisive action, and that at such times losses are necessary. He would never have such an opportunity again.

Wind and Rain. God commands the weather, and, incredibly, he brought weather patterns to favor the Americans at every stage of the Long Island campaign. On August 27 the northeast winds kept the British fleet from supporting Howe's ground attack and from moving into the East River to interdict Washington's communications and supply lines. As Howe waited for his naval support to come into action, the weather only got worse for the next two days. Torrential rains brought misery to both sides, but especially served to slow the British trench digging effort. This gave Washington vital time to plan and prepare for his retreat.

In the early evening of August 29 it became obvious that continuing wind and wave conditions would make the evacuation impossible. At the critical moment, the winds died. Suddenly, every boat could make the passage at full capacity, and the boatlift was no longer in jeopardy. As the weather changed, the British fleet made preparations to advance early on August 30. As dawn approached, however, another weather change would serve to keep the British ships at bay.

That Heavenly Messenger. Heavy fog in August was an unusual event for New York harbor. The almost impenetrable fog that settled over the water on August 30, 1776, was a well-documented occurrence. This phenomenon served to protect a large portion of Washington's army that evacuated during the daylight hours of that day, including General Washington himself, the last man to leave the island. He and his men were effectively screened from observation and fire as God acted again to protect the American army at its most vulnerable moment.

Sprechen sie Deutsch? Mrs. Repelye's Negro servant had a 75 percent chance of finding an Englishman during his midnight foray to warn of the American retreat. Instead, he was detained by Hessians. If he had delivered his message to anyone who could have understood it, or if the retreat was discovered in any other way, the results would have been disastrous. There was even a period of time when the Americans abandoned their entire line, which in itself should have alerted the British pickets. At that time a British unit could have walked through the empty lines. Any British attack or probe could have caused havoc within the confused colonial columns trying to move to the boat landings.

Chapter Eight
Trenton and Princeton

The Hessian colonel laughed. What a pathetic effort! The expected rebel attack had turned out to be almost comical. They had hit his northern outpost and inflicted a few casualties during a brief, but intense exchange of fire. The rebels had then retreated in disorder. By the time he was able to assemble his full regiment on the square in Trenton there was no one left to fight. The weather was miserable, and now he regretted keeping his troops on alert all Christmas Day for what he should have expected. Tomorrow he would send in his report that the anticipated rebel attack had been met and repulsed. Right now his men needed to get inside and enjoy some of the Christmas celebrations they had missed. He was looking forward himself to a warm fire, a good drink, and a friendly game of cards.

Colonel Johann Rall's Hessian brigade was part of a larger British force that had chased the American rebels for a month all the way across New Jersey. By late 1776 it seemed that there was no fight left in the rebels or their leader, George Washington. The war seemed to be coming to an end.

THE RETREAT GOES ON

The military situation did not improve for Washington and his army after they abandoned Long Island. The British

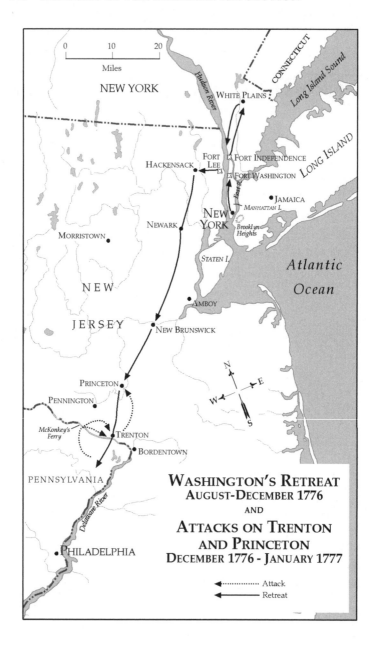

WASHINGTON'S RETREAT
AUGUST-DECEMBER 1776
AND
ATTACKS ON TRENTON
AND PRINCETON
DECEMBER 1776 - JANUARY 1777

············· Attack
——— Retreat

moved cautiously but inexorably forward, managing to avoid frontal assaults on prepared positions. They used ships to bypass strongpoints, moving farther up the Hudson and East rivers. By October 16 Washington was forced to abandon Manhattan.

The Continental Army retreated north toward Westchester and tried to establish another defensive line at White Plains. On the 28th Howe turned this position with another flanking movement, again coming close to destroying the Continental Army. On November 16 the British captured Fort Washington on the Hudson River, taking almost three thousand prisoners. Constantly guessing at Howe's intentions, Washington divided his forces, leaving 5,500 troops under General Charles Lee north of New York City to guard the main routes into New England. With the remainder of his forces he crossed the Hudson into New Jersey to defend against a thrust to the South and Philadelphia.

Washington immediately found himself faced by a well-equipped army of ten thousand British and Hessian troops under the command of General Charles Cornwallis. The defense of New Jersey soon turned into an escalating retreat through Hackensack, Newark, and Brunswick. Desertions and expiring enlistments plagued Washington's army. On November 30 almost two thousand militiamen from New Jersey and Maryland left the ranks. By December the colonials were at Trenton on the Delaware River with about three thousand men remaining in ranks. Most of these were only waiting for their enlistments to expire at year's end.

Washington wrote to his brother Augustine, "If every nerve is not strained to recruit the new army with all possible expedition, I think the game is pretty nearly up. . . . You can form no idea of the perplexity of my situation. No man, I believe, ever had a greater choice of difficulties, and less means to extricate himself from them."[198] Washington was about out of men and materiel. His supply situation was pitiful. Uniforms were nonexistent, and men had to wear whatever they could find to cover their bodies and feet. Sickness began to prey on exhausted, underfed, exposed, and demoralized troops.

Thomas Paine was with Washington's army during this period. At this point in the campaign he wrote the pamphlet *The American Crisis*, that began "These are the times that try men's souls. The summer soldier and sunshine patriot will, in this crisis, shrink from the service of his country; but he that stands it now, deserves the love and thanks of every man and woman."[199] In spite of Paine's eloquence, soldiers continued to disappear from the ranks.

FINAL COLLAPSE?

As Washington pulled his tattered army back across the Delaware on December 7, the new nation had quickly come to its darkest hour. The euphoria of the summer had given way to despair over the collapsing military situation. The British invasion force had taken on an aura of invincibility. Nothing lay between it and Philadelphia except a rapidly disappearing army and a river, which was already beginning to freeze over and would soon be no obstacle to advancing troops.

The political repercussions began to multiply. Feeling unsafe in Philadelphia, the Congress moved to Baltimore. Voices were heard criticizing General Washington for his failure to make a stand. Rumors circulated of a move to replace him with General Lee. Behind the advancing British lines, loyalist sentiment was growing throughout New Jersey and New York. General Howe encouraged this trend by issuing a proclamation of pardon on November 30 to all who would swear allegiance to the king. Thousands took advantage of the offer.[200] It seemed that the thirteen states were about to become twelve or even eleven. As Washington was being criticized, King George promoted Howe to full general and knighted him for his achievements.

For weeks General Washington had implored Charles Lee to rejoin the main army with the force assigned to him. Lee delayed and resisted complying with this order, as he had ambitions of his own to take over command of the Continental Army. His correspondence revealed a growing disdain for Washington's leadership. Then, in a peculiar and embarrassing incident, British dragoons captured Lee while he was at a tavern several miles from his command on December 13. The British rejoiced at this coup, and the Americans viewed it as a disaster, as Lee was one of the few experienced officers in the army.

DESPERATE MEASURES

In desperation Washington began to conceive a plan to recross the Delaware and to attack the Hessian garrison occupying Trenton. The Hessian brigade at Trenton consisted of three regiments of 1,400 veteran troops commanded by Colonel Johann Rall. Rall's Hessians had fought at Fort Washington and had accepted the surrender of the American forces captured there six weeks before. By the time they occupied Trenton, Colonel Rall and his troops were very high in self-confidence and quite low in their opinion of the Continental Army.

Washington's plan called for a force of 2,400 men under his own command to cross the river on Christmas night at McKonkey's Ferry, nine miles north of the town, and to strike Trenton before first light. This was not an overwhelming force to throw against a defended position. Most commanders would consider a numerical advantage of three to one barely adequate in such an attack. Washington was counting on Christmas

Washington Crossing the Delaware (painting by Emanuel Leutze—National Archives)

celebrations, darkness, and secrecy. He got unexpected help from some of the worst weather on record, which added a degree of safety, along with untold misery, to the venture.

Washington had to rely on complete and total surprise for any chance of success. Any warning or any degree of readiness among the Hessians would have spelled total disaster. The odds were decidedly against Washington as he took what can only be considered a desperate gamble. Although he used all the resources available and planned this action to the best of his ability, the outcome was not in his control. God's hand would be the critical factor at Washington's most desperate moment.

HESSIANS AT TRENTON

Since arriving in Trenton on December 12, Colonel Rall and his Hessian force had been busy. Rall intended to cross the river as soon as it was frozen and to move against Philadelphia.[201] While in Trenton, however, he had to focus considerable energy on maintaining his lines of communication against small bands of rebels appearing east of the Delaware. He sent patrols out from Trenton, several of which encountered and exchanged fire with colonials. His immediate superior, Colonel Von Donop, was concerned with this activity and instructed Rall to put up fortifications. He also assigned an engineer to assist in the task.[202]

Rall chose to ignore these instructions. When his own second in command, Major Von Dechow, and other subordinates urged the same precautions, he exclaimed, "Let them come! We want no trenches! We'll at them with the bayonet!"[203] He also proclaimed that he would soon be crossing the ice to advance on Philadelphia. Rall agreed only to outposts on the roads leading into town. His contempt for the colonial army had begun influencing his judgment.

In spite of the secrecy used by Washington in his preparations, Rall began hearing rumors and reports of rebel activity several days before Christmas. Two deserters warned that militia units were gathering in Pennsylvania and had prepared several days' rations.[204] On December 23 Dr. William Bryant, who lived near Trenton, sought out Colonel Rall to tell him of a report from a Negro who had just crossed the river. He brought information that rebels were drawing rations and preparing to attack Trenton.[205] On Christmas Day General James Grant at Princeton forwarded an intelligence report warning of an attack that day.[206] Although he continued to downplay these warnings, Rall ensured that one of his regiments was under arms and alert on Christmas Day.

During the day on December 25 Colonel Rall went about his usual garrison routine. In the morning he inspected his men on parade and enjoyed the martial music played by his band.[207] After checking outposts around the outskirts of town in the afternoon he returned to his quarters for a game of checkers with his host, Stacy Potts.

At about seven o'clock that evening firing broke out on the north side of town. A report came in that the outpost on Pennington Road was under attack. The entire garrison in Trenton was immediately in an uproar. Colonel Rall sent reinforcements to the outpost and assembled his regiment on the north side of town. Soon he began receiving reports. He learned that about thirty rebel troops had attacked the outpost and wounded six of his men. When fire was returned, the rebels had broken off the attack. A patrol had gone up the Pennington Road about two miles but had found nothing.

Major Von Dechow recommended a more extensive reconnaissance around Trenton.[208] Rall vetoed this proposal. He assumed that the predicted rebel attack had occurred. His contempt for the colonials only grew over this pitiful effort. He returned to Trenton to resume the Christmas revelry. Returning to town, Rall ordered a stand down of his troops and allowed them to return to quarters in light of the miserable weather. He himself decided to join a Christmas party at Abraham Hunt's house, where he was able to play cards and drink into the night.

Later in the evening a Tory farmer from Bucks County, Pennsylvania, knocked on the door and asked a servant to see Colonel Rall. The servant would not let him in, telling him that the colonel was too busy to see anyone. The farmer wrote out a note explaining that the whole American army was crossing the river and marching on Trenton. His duty done, the farmer left and disappeared into the night. The servant delivered the note,

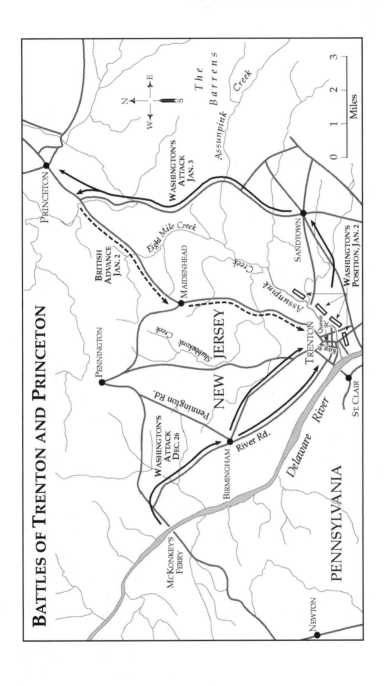

BATTLES OF TRENTON AND PRINCETON

which Rall put into his pocket unread as he continued playing cards.[209]

Unfortunately for him, he was not able to read the note written in English and felt no need to bother with a translation. Someone found the note the next day in the same pocket as Colonel Rall was dying. When informed of its contents he said, "If I had read this . . . I would not be here now."[210] If he had read the note, events of the next day would have unfolded in a vastly different way.

THE BATTLE OF TRENTON

Totally unaware of these miraculous events working in his favor, Washington commenced his second crossing of the Delaware late on Christmas Day. To negotiate the ice-filled river Washington again turned to Colonel John Glover and his brigade of Massachusetts seamen. Using locally available 40–60 foot Durham boats, Glover's men began to ferry Washington's troops and artillery across the river as soon as it was dark. A storm of wind, sleet, and snow raged throughout the night causing untold suffering among the ill-clad troops and Washington himself.

The plan called for completion of the crossing by midnight, allowing for a five-hour march to Trenton and a predawn attack. The movement fell dangerously behind schedule due to the weather and state of the river. By 4:00 a.m. Washington's forces were finally across the river and advancing toward Trenton along two roads.[211] Every man was half frozen, completely soaked, and certain that his musket would not fire. Even knowing the condition of his men and loss of darkness for cover, Washington pressed on.

At about 7:45 the first outposts were encountered and quickly driven in. The attack continued into Trenton. Surprise was complete as the Hessian units were caught in total confusion. Their

Battle of Trenton (engraving by Illman Brothers—National Archives)

officers assembled units piecemeal and fought isolated engagements throughout the town. The American artillery, so laboriously brought across the river, proved decisive as it was brought
into action at the head of the two main streets. Although musket
fire was intermittent, cannon fire boomed down King and Queen
streets, breaking up attempted Hessian counterattacks.[212] Colonel
Rall himself tried to rally his men on the south side of town but
was mortally wounded. By 9:00 a.m. Hessian units were surren-
dering or fleeing to the south. The battle was over.

In a few hours Washington had broken a Hessian brigade
and had captured nine hundred prisoners and a stockpile of
equipment, small arms, and artillery.[213] Several hundred escaped
before the encirclement of the town was complete. The captives
gazed in wonder at the bedraggled state of their conquerors. The
Americans had lost two men frozen during the night. Two officers and one enlisted man were wounded. One of the wounded

officers was Lieutenant James Monroe, destined to be a future president.[214]

It had been Washington's plan to continue on the offensive after taking Trenton. However, some of his units never made it across the river during the night. His men at Trenton were in no condition to do more. Washington marched his spent troops and the captured Hessians back to McKonkey's Ferry to cross the Delaware again later on the same day as the battle. There was no abatement of the fierce weather. Three more men froze to death in the boats. Washington found little time to speculate on what his army had accomplished.

BATTLE OF PRINCETON

Three days later Washington took his forces back across the Delaware. With the remnants of his army and reinforcements from the

Hessians Surrender at Trenton (copy of lithograph—National Archives)

Pennsylvania militia he assembled about five thousand men and forty artillery pieces in Trenton. The militia units were untrained and inexperienced, and the physical condition of his own men had not improved noticeably. This was another extremely risky move by Washington, who must have known that the British would react strongly to his attack on Trenton. In spite of the danger, Washington resolved to continue with his original plan to move on Princeton and beyond. On January 1 he sent advance units to a position about five miles outside Trenton, or roughly halfway to Princeton.

Unknown to Washington, General Cornwallis had quickly assembled a force of eight thousand men in Princeton. Washington was familiar with the slow and methodical Howe, and did not yet grasp how fast a more energetic general could react to changing circumstances. This was a dangerous miscalculation on his part, as he would learn the next day.

Leaving a security force under Lieutenant Colonel Charles Mawhood at Princeton, Cornwallis advanced toward Trenton on January 2. During the night of January 1 there had been heavy rain and high temperatures for January, and the roads were deep in mud. Terrible road conditions and well-fought delaying actions by Washington's lead units slowed the British advance. It was late in the afternoon before the British column reached the outskirts of Trenton.

Forced to pull back in the face of this powerful force, Washington consolidated his entire command and took up defensive positions along a ridgeline just south of Assunpink Creek. As darkness set in, Cornwallis had his units make camp to wait for the next day. By this time it had become clear to Washington that he was in another desperate situation. A superior force was in front of him. Assunpink Creek was easily fordable and no obstacle to an attack. The Delaware River was to his rear. Retreat across the river would be a disaster with enemy forces so close.

Washington was saved by local knowledge of the roads and a bold plan. That night he held a council of his officers to consider options. There seemed to be no attractive solution to their predicament. Then someone suggested the possibility of skirting the British lines by moving on a new road to the east that would enable them to approach Princeton from the south.[215] This idea posed many risks, but captured everyone's imagination in its boldness. Washington ordered immediate preparations.

By this time Washington's troops had mastered the art of retreating. Once again, they had to cautiously disengage from an enemy force in close contact. In this case much of the movement was parallel to the enemy's lines and even more susceptible to detection. Officers enforced strict noise discipline among the troops. No talking or commands were allowed above a whisper. Wagon wheels were padded to make them quieter. A rear guard of four hundred men stayed behind to keep up the campfires and to continue the appearance and sound of digging along the lines.

As Washington's units prepared to move, a major obstacle to his plan disappeared. Early in the evening the wind shifted to the northwest and the temperature began to fall. This added to the troops' misery, but also caused a hard freeze of the roads.[216] The wagons and artillery could move freely again, and Washington's entire column was able to make good time after getting under way at around one the next morning.

Early on January 3, 1777, the lead American units reached the outskirts of Princeton and quickly engaged Mawhood's force of three regiments. An intense fight developed. Washington repeatedly came under enemy fire as he moved to the front to rally his men. In heavy fighting his units drove the British back and split their force. Some retreated toward Trenton, while others moved toward New Brunswick. British casualties amounted to 273, while the Americans lost forty killed and about one hundred wounded.[217] The Americans captured over two hundred prisoners.[218] For the moment Washington was in possession of Princeton.

Knowing that time was precious, Washington quickly decided his next move. His troops were exhausted and in no condition for further offensive action. He reluctantly ordered a march to the wooded hill country around Morristown, where an encampment was already prepared. The outmaneuvered Cornwallis arrived in Princeton in time to see the rebels' rear guard moving out of town. He then moved his force to New Brunswick, thinking that the rebels were threatening that base. Washington had made another successful escape.

GOD'S HAND AT TRENTON AND PRINCETON

In December 1776 the fire of revolution was almost extinguished. New York and New Jersey were firmly in the hands of British forces. Congress had abandoned Philadelphia, and it lay unprotected before the British advance. There was practically nothing left of the so-called Continental Army, which was about to completely cease to exist with expiring enlistments. As far as the British and many Americans were concerned, the rebellion and so-called war would soon be over.

The battles at Trenton and Princeton completely changed this picture. After Washington moved to Morristown, he established a defensive enclave for the winter from which he could harass British supply lines through New Jersey. Washington's success emboldened local citizens to retaliate against the Hessian and British troops who had abused them during their months of occupation. British supply and troop movements were harassed everywhere. Howe had to abandon most of New Jersey except for New Brunswick and Perth Amboy, which he could resupply by water from New York. Within these few days the war had taken on a completely new character.

News spread rapidly to the rest of the country. Confidence in George Washington and the Continental Army took an upward turn. Suddenly it became easier to recruit new companies and regiments in the states. The commissary officers found it a little easier to collect food and supplies. People would at least consider taking Continental currency again. The Congress moved back to Philadelphia.[219]

When news reached England, the reaction was shock and disillusionment. It was suddenly obvious that there would be no quick end to the war. Requests came in from Howe for twenty thousand more troops and for more ships to shore up an unsuccessful blockade. During the successes of the summer and fall, opposition to the war had fallen silent in Parliament. Whig supporters of the colonies began to find their voice. William Pitt made a famous speech to the House of Lords warning of the danger of France entering the war and reiterating the justness of the American cause. Pitt called the war, "Unjust in its principles, impracticable in its means, and ruinous in its consequences."[220]

The resolve of the king and British government did not disappear, although the problems in prosecuting a distant and increasingly unpopular war had suddenly escalated. Winston Churchill, as a historian, would comment, "The effect of the stroke was out of all proportion to its military importance. It was the most critical moment in the war."[221]

The impact of Trenton and Princeton was also felt in France. At first the French government had viewed the American Revolution with uncertainty. There was considerable pleasure over England's difficulties and a constant search for opportunities to benefit from the conflict. However, there was reluctance on the part of the king to openly support a rebellion against another Crown. France also could not afford a direct military confrontation with England due to the weakness of her navy and vulnerability of her shipping.

In early 1776 Silas Deane, a member of Congress, went to Paris to seek assistance for the American war effort. He got it in the form of a clandestine operation through a fictitious company called Hortalez et Cie.[222] Through this company quantities of clothing and ammunition were secretly forwarded to America and were extremely helpful to Washington during the early stages of the war. In December 1776 Benjamin Franklin arrived in Paris to join with Deane in seeking not only aid but also an alliance with France. This would not happen for another year, but events at Trenton and Princeton gave credibility to the diplomats' efforts.

Washington deserves great credit for his generalship in these battles. His success in crossing the Delaware on Christmas night can be contrasted with the failure of his other commanders to accomplish the same feat under the same conditions. Washington was resolute, and he instilled the same quality in those around him. He was determined to do whatever he could to alter the course of a losing effort.

In his determination, however, Washington took several gambles that jeopardized his army. Except for the amazing protection of God's providential hand at critical moments, he would have lost his army and jeopardized the Revolution in the final days of 1776.

Friday the Thirteenth. The outright capture of a general officer on the battlefield is a rare occurrence. Lee's capture on December 13 was a strange affair, combining a peculiar lapse in judgment on his own part and fortuitous information falling into British hands. The loss of Washington's second in command fueled the already growing panic in the Congress, and gave the British cause for further confidence in the military situation. However, one historian more correctly termed this amazing incident the "Luckiest Friday the Thirteenth in History."[223] The immediate beneficial result was to remove a growing and misguided challenge to Washington's authority and to see Lee's two thousand troops speedily returned to Washington's control by General John Sullivan. Miraculously, Washington was able for the first time in months to consider the possibility of offensive action.

The Phantom Attack. Up until the time of the small engagement on Christmas afternoon, the Hessians were prepared for Washington's attack. The perfect timing of this incident led Colonel Rall to conclude that the predicted attack had taken place. The identity of the Americans who participated remains a mystery. Several historians contend that a patrol from a Virginia regiment made the probe of the Hessian outpost.[224] Another cited an advance party returning from New Jersey.[225] Others could only speculate that these were local farmers on a rampage over some grievance with the unpopular Hessians, or that they were a band of rebels.[226] The identity of those involved is less important than the miraculous timing of this incident, which had a decisive effect on Hessian preparedness and the battle to follow.

The Unopened Note. Later Christmas evening Rall received another clear warning of Washington's approach. The Tory farmer went to a lot of trouble to reach Trenton with his news. It would have taken Rall only minutes to listen to his report. Failing that, he could have had the note translated and read by someone while the cards were being dealt. This professional Hessian officer was not lazy or inefficient. His success as a combat commander had been proven repeatedly. This unusual lapse can be best understood as another miracle protecting Washington's army during its most vulnerable moment.

Amazing Weather. On January 2 Cornwallis was mired in mud on an unseasonably warm day. This was an important factor in his slow advance on Trenton. If he had arrived earlier in the day, Washington's weak position on the Assunpink would have been even weaker. A battle on that day in that location would have been disastrous for the Americans. Miraculously, that same night the temperature dropped in time to expedite Washington's movement around Cornwallis. The Americans had a very brief window of opportunity for success at Princeton. If they had arrived later in the day, they could have again faced Cornwallis's entire force and a disastrous battle.

Chapter Nine
Saratoga

Baroness Von Riedesel had heard General Burgoyne state emphatically, "The British never retreat." Accompanying her husband, General Friedrich Von Riedesel, on Burgoyne's invasion of New York, she had witnessed a triumphal march since leaving Canada. She could not believe what was happening now. On this night, October 8, 1777, she was cold, wet, and afraid. In her words, "We drove on all through the night. Little Frederika, was very much frightened, often starting to cry, and I had to hold my handkerchief over her mouth to prevent our being discovered." The next day, "Toward evening we finally reached Saratoga . . . I was wet to the skin from the rain and had to remain so throughout the night as there was no place to change into dry clothes."[227] The baroness was an eyewitness to one of the greatest changes of fortune in military history.

AT THE START of 1777, General John Burgoyne was in England advocating a plan to win the war in America. He wanted to attack the colonies from Canada, take Fort Ticonderoga, and advance down the Hudson River. With General Howe supporting from the south the colonies would be split and the rebel army crushed.

At this time George Washington had positioned his battered army around Morristown, New Jersey, where he could harass

British supply lines and try to rebuild his forces. General Howe remained in New York City with the troops and shipping to strike anywhere. Washington could only wonder where this would be.

THE GRAND STRATEGY

The British high command had discussed a so-called Grand Strategy for some time. Separating New England from the other colonies along the line of the Hudson River had been an underlying strategic goal of Howe's campaign to take New York City in 1776. In October and again in November Howe wrote to Lord George Germain, the secretary of state for the colonies in London, stating his intention of "opening a communication with Canada" during 1777.[228] Germain accordingly proceeded with plans to facilitate the strategy.

The water was muddied on February 23 when Germain received another letter from Howe written on December 20 indicating an unexpected change of mind. Howe would focus his main effort for the year on Philadelphia, the rebel capitol. Referring to the northern campaign, he stated, "There may be a corps to act defensively upon the lower part of the Hudson River, to cover Jersey on that side, as well as to facilitate, in some degree, the approach of the army from Canada."[229] In Howe's mind any activity in the north would be a sideshow.

Inexplicably, Germain wrote to Howe on March 9 approving his plans, without even referring to the northern campaign.[230] Shortly afterward, on March 26, he actually issued orders for that operation, giving General John Burgoyne the mission of forcing his way to Albany from Canada and calling for the "most speedy junction of the two armies."[231]

The principals thus created a serious ambiguity in the Grand Strategy and allowed it to fester. Historians have pinned the blame in varying degrees on Germain, Howe, and Burgoyne. Each had motives of his own and clear failures at this and later stages of the campaign. At this point, however, the direct responsibility falls on Germain. He could have settled the matter with clear orders to Howe. For whatever reason, he never saw fit to countermand Howe's plans or to even stress the importance of Burgoyne's operation.

One prejudice that colored the thinking of the entire British high command was an underestimation of their enemy. They did not foresee that American military units could seriously impede British advances on any front, even if high-level coordination was imperfect. Burgoyne was in London during this exchange of correspondence and even consulted with Germain as he prepared the orders for the expedition.[232] He was not too concerned at the time about any ambiguity in the plan. With supreme confidence and his commission as a lieutenant general, he departed on March 27 for his month-long voyage to Canada.

AMERICAN FORCES

Washington in New Jersey. George Washington had little time to savor his successes at Trenton and Princeton. He counted approximately three thousand effective troops left in his army at Morristown, where he remained in a defensive posture from January to May 1777. He was able to harass British posts and supply lines in New Jersey to some degree but spent most of his energies in trying to recruit and reorganize.

Washington was also preoccupied with determining the intentions of General Howe in New York. Howe was capable

Portrait of Philip Schuyler (painting by John Trumbull— National Archives)

of attacking in any direction, by land or sea, and Washington had to try to be ready for anything. Although he worried about potential threats from Canada he was not in a position to think much or to do much about them.

The North. The Continental Congress had appointed Philip Schuyler to the rank of major general in 1775, giving him command of the Northern Department and responsibility for the defense of upstate New York. Schuyler was a wealthy landowner of Dutch descent with military experience in the region during the French and Indian War. In early 1777 Schuyler had an inadequate assortment of militia and Continental units on hand to cover a vast region that included the most likely invasion route from Canada, along Lake Champlain and the Hudson River.

Fort Ticonderoga lay at the foot of Lake Champlain and had been a key military outpost for decades. Originally designed to defend against an attack from the south, it was now in the hands of the Americans and was considered a bulwark against invasion from the north. Unfortunately, reality did not live up to this impression. The fort had fallen into a serious state of disrepair and was manned by a poorly equipped force of only 1,700 men.

In March 1777 Schuyler requested ten thousand troops from General Washington to defend Ticonderoga and another two thousand for the Mohawk River valley.[233] Washington had no means to comply with this request. Since he had never visited Ticonderoga he overestimated its defensibility, and he also thought that the main British threat would come from New York City rather than from Canada. For some time to come Schuyler would be on his own.

BURGOYNE'S CAMPAIGN

Forces. Implementation of the Grand Strategy began with great fanfare on June 13, 1777. An impressive naval force of 28 gunboats sailed south from St. John, followed by two hundred flat-bottomed bateaux carrying infantry and artillery. Over seven thousand troops were embarked, about half British regulars and half German mercenaries.

The expedition was exceptionally heavy in artillery, with 138 large caliber weapons ranging from twenty-four pounders to 4.4-inch mortars.[234] Having seen the action at Bunker Hill the year before, Burgoyne did not intend to be caught short in any confrontation with the rebels. Prodigious quantities of ammunition and stores were embarked to support these weapons.

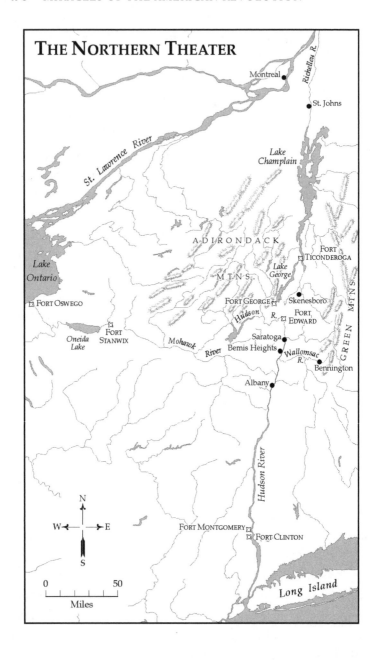

THE NORTHERN THEATER

Augmenting these forces were a few hundred Canadians and American Tories. These were far fewer than the number expected. Burgoyne assumed that many loyalists would join his ranks, especially as he liberated areas to the south. In this he would be continually disappointed.

A group of about four hundred Indians also joined the expedition and would prove a mixed blessing. The Indians made superior scouts and advance guards, but were difficult, and at times impossible, to control. They frequently ran wild in attacking and plundering soldiers and civilians alike. Indian atrocities would cause Burgoyne a lot of trouble.

Fall of Ticonderoga. By July 2 Burgoyne's forces had moved down Lake Champlain and were in position to attack Fort Ticonderoga. His immediate goal was to capture the fort and its garrison. After probing the defenses for several days, a British officer discovered to his amazement that a key terrain feature was not occupied. Sugarloaf Hill was about 1,500 yards southwest of the main American fort and provided a position dominating the fort. When the British moved troops and artillery into position on top of the hill, the battle was basically decided.

At this point the American commander, General Arthur St. Clair, faced a terrible decision. He knew that his defenses would not be able to hold indefinitely with Sugarloaf Hill occupied by the British. With each hour his force was in greater danger of being completely cut off from retreat. How long should he continue to fight? Only dishonor awaited the commander who surrendered Fort Ticonderoga, actually referred to at the time as "The Gibraltar of the North."

On July 5 St. Clair made his decision. He abandoned all of his positions that night, moving some of his force by water down Lake George and the rest overland by a circular route south to Fort Edward. By this time, the escape was narrow and pursuit by the

British immediate. By swiftly advancing across the lake, the British captured practically all of the Americans' carefully evacuated stores, ammunition, and artillery. This was a considerable disaster for the Americans. However, the British failed to cut off St. Clair's retreat, frustrating one of Burgoyne's primary goals. When the retreating Americans finally reached Fort Edward, they were able to more than double Schuyler's available forces for the fights to come.

Loss of Fort Ticonderoga sent shock waves throughout the colonies and resulted in St. Clair's court-martial.[235] Much of the blame also fell on Philip Schuyler, who found his command position in jeopardy in spite of his otherwise sound leadership in an untenable situation.

Rejoicing erupted in England when word of the fort's capture arrived on August 22. John Burgoyne was the hero of the hour. The king himself suggested a knighthood for the victorious general but was persuaded to wait a while longer before bestowing this honor.[236]

A Bad Omen. On July 13 the triumphant Burgoyne set up his headquarters in Skenesboro where he settled in for a prolonged pause to build up supplies for the next advance. A few days later a force of about five hundred Indian warriors from tribes of the Iroquois League arrived in Burgoyne's camp to join the army that seemed to be winning the war.[237] These warriors were fierce fighters and were able to wreak havoc on the retreating Americans. Unfortunately, they did not confine their fury to combatants.

On July 27 an incident occurred with profound ramifications. An Ottawa Indian named Wyandot Panther brutally killed and scalped a twenty-three-year-old woman named Jane McCrea.[238] She had been engaged to a Tory officer serving with Burgoyne. This story became a sensation throughout New York and New England as it was told, retold, and published in papers. Jane McCrea became a rallying cry, stirring militia units to action throughout the region.[239]

Burgoyne himself was horrified at this incident. His efforts to bring the killer to justice and to reign in his Indian allies had the result of disaffecting the Indians. Soon they began to disappear in increasing numbers until, by early August, Burgoyne found he had lost his accustomed eyes and ears.

Wilderness. When the time came to advance from Skenesboro, Burgoyne faced an important decision. He had earlier planned to advance by water down Lake George where the overland portage to the Hudson River was about ten miles over a well-traveled route. Unexpectedly, he decided instead to strike directly south through twenty miles of dense wilderness. With the wild country and rebel working parties impeding his progress, he managed to advance at the rate of about one mile per day.[240]

It was not until early August that Burgoyne reached Fort Edward on the Hudson, already abandoned by Schuyler's forces. Here, he made another extensive pause of several weeks to wait for his supplies to catch up and to try to solve some of his growing logistics problems with a foraging expedition of his own.

No Help from Howe. On August 3 a British officer arrived at Burgoyne's headquarters with a long awaited message from General Howe.[241] The news was not what Burgoyne expected or hoped to hear. Howe announced his departure from New York City with the objective of taking Philadelphia. For the first time Burgoyne had to face the reality of his campaign's strategic flaw. There would be no grand union of British armies at Albany or even very much cooperation between them.

SCHUYLER'S RETREAT

After Ticonderoga the northern army faced a desperate situation. Even with St. Clair's troops back within his ranks, General Schuyler could muster only about four thousand men, unfortunately in various states of disorganization. Loss of the artillery, ammunition, and stores so carefully built up at Ticonderoga was a severe blow. Schuyler did all that he could. He sent correspondence to every quarter pleading for help and set about delaying Burgoyne's advance in every way possible.

Schuyler's soldiers turned into lumberjacks and wrecking crews. They blocked roads and trails with fallen trees, boulders, and even streams that they diverted. Every bridge was dismantled or burned. Crops were cut or burned, and livestock driven off. General Schuyler even had his own wheat fields around Saratoga torched.[242] This work was dangerous in itself due to almost constant attack by bands of Indians.

During July Schuyler's strength fluctuated from day to day as a few new units came in and others departed in spite of pleas that they stay. Morale was about as low as it could go for men doing such dangerous and backbreaking manual labor, all the while retreating from the enemy. They could only hope that the tide would somehow turn.

On August 10 General Schuyler's service came to an inglorious end. A dispatch arrived from John Hancock, president of Congress, relieving him of command and directing that he and General St. Clair report to General Washington's headquarters, presumably to face court-martial.[243] To make matters worse Congress replaced him with an old antagonist, Horatio Gates.

GATES IN COMMAND

Horatio Gates served in the British army during the French and Indian War and was wounded on the day of Braddock's debacle on the Monongahela, described in chapter four. After his discharge from the service he stayed in Virginia where he maintained contact with his old comrade-in-arms, George

Washington. In 1775 Washington nominated him to serve as his adjutant general. Gates was a capable administrator, but had already given Washington doubt about his ability to command. Due mainly to his carefully cultivated political support, Gates now found that he was at the war's center of action.

Gates was to be the immediate beneficiary of events over which he had little control. Burgoyne's supply problems, slowing advance, and loss of Indian allies have already been mentioned. In addition, developments to the east and west would have profound effects on the American defense of the Hudson.

Bennington. On August 11 Burgoyne sent one of his German officers, Lieutenant Colonel Frederick Baum, and a detachment of about eight hundred men on a major foraging expedition around Bennington (now in Vermont). Scouts had reported that desperately needed horses were available there and that rebel forces were scarce.

Unknown to the British, however, the New Hampshire legislature had raised a brigade of militia during July and given command of it to John Stark, one of the heroes of Bunker Hill. Stark's 1,500-man force was tasked with the defense of New Hampshire and its western frontier against any threat from Burgoyne's army.[244]

Stark's units met the advancing Hessians west of Bennington on August 14, and a full-scale battle followed two days later along the Walloomsac River. At about 5:00 p.m., after a fierce fight in which Baum was mortally wounded, the Hessians surrendered en masse. Within minutes another column of Hessians sent in relief arrived on the battlefield. After another sharp engagement, Stark's men also routed this force.

The march of this Hessian relief force to Bennington was a drama of its own. Heavy rains turned the only road into a quagmire. Lieutenant Colonel Heinrich Breymann, the commander of the relief force, seemed possessed with the need to move all his artillery and stores and to keep his units in formation. He let precious time pass with frequent stops to close ranks and reorganize. On this march he managed to advance at the rate of about one mile per hour.[245] If he had arrived on the battlefield an hour sooner, the history of the battle and campaign would have been written differently.

In this small, but decisive, engagement Burgoyne lost one thousand of his best troops with their weapons and equipment. More importantly, he failed completely to resupply his own army at this critical juncture. This little victory also provided the first glimmer of hope to a retreating army and demoralized populace.

Fort Stanwix. At about the same time, another drama was playing out on Gates's other flank, over eighty miles to the west. Fort Stanwix stood on the far western frontier guarding the approach to the Mohawk River valley. Another British force commanded by Colonel Barry St. Leger had departed Montreal in June. With about 1000 men St. Leger's mission was to support Burgoyne's advance by attacking along the Mohawk. By early August this force had reached Fort Stanwix.

St. Leger found the fort defended by about five hundred Continental troops who successfully held off his first attacks. The British were forced to mount a siege, which went on for several weeks. In a bold move General Schuyler depleted his own inadequate command to send a relief force under Benedict Arnold. On August 23, as Arnold approached, St. Leger abandoned his attack and withdrew to Canada.

The bad news from Ft. Stanwix reached Burgoyne by Indian courier on August 28.[246] The support and diversion that he had been expecting from this quarter disappeared.

New Troops. During August the population of New England and surrounding areas began to stir. Jane McCrea's death was a factor. Also, there was a slowly growing sense that the tide was turning on the Hudson. Men were pouring into militia units to march against the British and Burgoyne. Gates himself can be credited with some of this enthusiasm as he seemed to inspire more confidence than the aristocratic and discredited Schuyler. By early September Gates's forces totaled over six thousand, approaching parity with his enemy.[247]

Of special note was the arrival in Gates's camp of Colonel Daniel Morgan and his elite unit of sharpshooters. These men were known for their Kentucky rifles and expert marksmanship. Morgan himself was a fierce fighter who had distinguished himself earlier at Quebec.

Other Continental units joined Gates's forces. John Glover arrived with his Massachusetts regiment, which had served with such distinction at Long Island and Trenton. On September 1 Benedict Arnold returned from the Mohawk with his force of 1,200 men.[248]

THE BATTLE OF FREEMAN'S FARM[249]

Burgoyne Crosses the Rubicon. By early September Burgoyne's grand procession down central New York had turned into a very cautious advance. His combat power was largely intact and still represented a potent force. However, his supply lines grew longer and more difficult to maintain against rebel raids. Local foraging was mostly unproductive, and it was obvious by this time that he could not count on other forces for assistance.

Burgoyne finally had to face a defining moment in his career. He still had the option of moving back to Fort Edward or even Fort George where he could solidify his logistic support and wait for help from some other quarter. His only other option was to cross the Hudson River,[250] cut himself off from his bases in Canada, and strike directly for Albany.

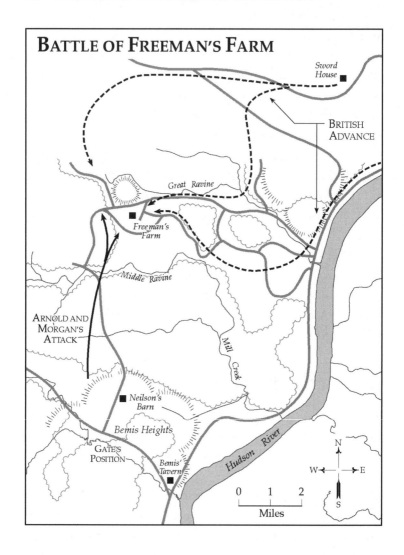

BATTLE OF FREEMAN'S FARM

Sword House

BRITISH ADVANCE

Great Ravine

Freeman's Farm

Middle Ravine

ARNOLD AND MORGAN'S ATTACK

Mill Creek

Neilson's Barn

Bemis Heights

GATE'S POSITION

Bemis' Tavern

Hudson River

0   1   2
Miles

N
W — E
S

John Burgoyne was known to be something of a gambler. He was also an ambitious man with a keen concern for his own reputation. He knew that his reputation would not survive anything that others would perceive as turning back. It was probably not even a difficult decision. If he were going to wait for support, he would wait in Albany. He knew that he had to fight a decisive battle, and he still had supreme confidence in his troops and in himself. A battle would decide the issue, and he felt that in a battle the odds were on his side.

On September 13 Burgoyne took his army across the Hudson over a temporary boat bridge constructed a few miles north of Saratoga. The bridge was then dismantled as the move south continued. His force was now about equal in numbers to the rebels,[251] but was superior in every other category.

The Americans Dig In. On September 7 General Gates issued orders that sent a wave of excitement throughout his army. The time had come to move north. For the first time in two months the northern army would no longer have its back to the enemy. Gates had a fairly clear picture of Burgoyne's situation and knew that he would have to fight a decisive battle if he did not retreat soon.

Accepting good advice from local residents and his own staff, Gates chose an extremely good defensive position at a place known as Bemis Heights.[252] Here a broad plateau overlooking the river dominated the road along the riverbank. Artillery could cover the road effectively from this position. To approach the heights, infantry would have to maneuver inland from the river over thickly wooded terrain cut by steep ravines and creeks. There were farms and cleared fields scattered through the area. This was not ideal terrain for Burgoyne's disciplined formations.

As he waited for Burgoyne's advance, Gates had about a week to prepare trenches and earthworks across a three-quarter-mile front. He placed his troops in good positions and waited for Burgoyne to come to him. In another wise and fortuitous decision, Gates placed the left wing of his defense under Benedict Arnold. Arnold was one of the most controversial figures of this war due to his later treason. However, at this stage, he had proven himself a highly effective field commander with distinguished service at Ticonderoga, Quebec, and Ft. Stanwix.

The Battle. At 8:00 a.m. on September 19 General Burgoyne launched a three-pronged attack on the rebel lines at Bemis Heights. His German units moved on the left along the river under the command of General Von Riedesel. The British units comprised the center and right attacks, with Burgoyne himself accompanying the center. Movement away from the river was exceedingly difficult as the infantry formations and artillery units traversed the steep ravines and heavy woods.

By this time the British had few Indian scouts, and the flow of battlefield information was very much in the favor of the Americans. Arnold's pickets soon detected the British deployment. As the situation progressed, Arnold perceived that his lines would be threatened if enemy forces gained the high ground to the west. Artillery fire from this area would be devastating in support of a ground attack. If his lines were penetrated, there might be no regrouping.

Although Gates preferred to wait in position for the British attack, Arnold suggested and then strongly pushed for an attack of his own. Gates reluctantly agreed to some of the best advice ever received by a commander in the field.

Daniel Morgan's riflemen advanced in the early afternoon and were the first to engage the British in and around a clearing known as Freeman's Farm. Their accurate rifle fire took a heavy toll on the British ranks, especially the officers.[253] One of the most intense fights of the war developed as commanders on both sides committed more units to the action. All afternoon the battle raged back and forth across the field with neither side able to consolidate an advantage. Time, distance, and the hesitancy of each commander prevented many units from becoming engaged in the fight.

Von Riedesel's troops finally decided the issue when they reached the scene, forcing the Americans back for the last time. Burgoyne's exhausted troops held the field, technically the victors. Burgoyne realized, however, that he had failed in his larger purpose. He had not come close to the rebel main line and had not achieved a breakthrough. The way was not open to Albany. As one British officer on the scene put it, "We have gained little more by our victory than honour."[254]

THE SECOND BATTLE

Trench Warfare. Burgoyne was strongly inclined to renew the battle on the next day but was dissuaded by his subordinates, who convinced him that the troops needed time to recover from their exertions. An attack was therefore set for September 21.

At this time the Americans were in even greater disarray than the British. Many units were disorganized, and ammunition was in critically short supply. For several days the Americans were on constant alert for the expected and feared main attack. Although Burgoyne did not realize it at the time, his last, best opportunity slipped away with the arrival of a messenger.

Before dawn on September 21 a courier from General Clinton finally reached Burgoyne's headquarters. A message drafted on September 12 stated in part, "If you think that two thousand

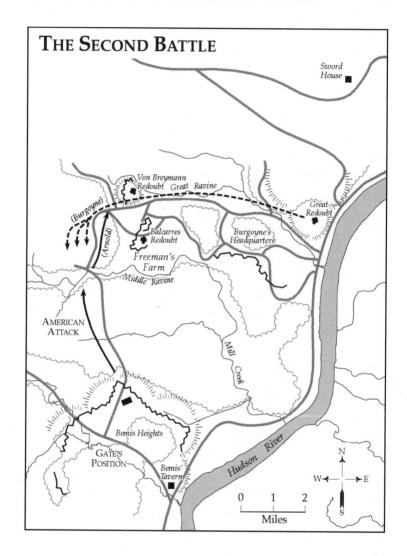

THE SECOND BATTLE

Sword House

Von Breymann Redoubt   Great Ravine

(Burgoyne)

Great Redoubt

(Arnold)

Balcarres Redoubt

Burgoyne's Headquarters

Freeman's Farm

Middle Ravine

AMERICAN ATTACK

Mill Creek

Bemis Heights

GATE'S POSITION

Bemis' Tavern

Hudson River

N
W   E
S

0   1   2
Miles

men can assist you effectually, I will make a push at (Fort) Montgomery in about ten days."[255] On the basis of this rather ambiguous information Burgoyne surrendered the initiative of his offensive campaign.

In anticipation of support from the south, Burgoyne undertook construction of his own defensive positions. His units dug a trench line connecting three strong points: the Great Redoubt on the left, the Balcarres Redoubt in the center near Freeman's farm, and the Breymann Redoubt on the far right. The British Grand Strategy had finally evolved into trench warfare.

Unfortunately for the British, several weeks of stalemate saw the American ranks swell, as new militia units arrived almost daily. By early October Gates's forces were around eight thousand and growing.[256] Gates was able to be much more aggressive in probing and harassing the British lines, keeping up a constant pressure. He also sent units north of the British position to cut off movement in that direction.

On October 3 Burgoyne had to order half rations for his command.[257] His troops, especially the sick and wounded, were also suffering from cold nights and inadequate clothing. Horses were dying from lack of forage. As supplies grew critically short, he had to face the fact that he could not afford to wait much longer for help from Clinton.[258]

Arnold. After the first battle, Generals Arnold and Gates became involved in an open and venomous dispute. In his report to Congress, Gates omitted mention of Arnold's actions during the battle, and this precipitated a bitter argument. Gates finally rearranged his leadership assignments, effectively leaving Arnold without a command. Reminiscent of Achilles before Troy, Arnold sulked in his quarters for days.

The Final Battle. In council on October 4 Burgoyne was unable to convince his officers of the wisdom of an all-out attack. There was even sentiment for a retreat, which he would not consider. Consequently, on October 7 Burgoyne undertook a strange and apparently desperate operation that was something less than an attack but more than a reconnaissance.

At about 10:00 a.m. he sent out a force of about one thousand men toward the American left. Gates reacted immediately to this movement by sending units against the flanks and front of Burgoyne's force. After a sharp engagement, the British were driven back into their lines. The affair might have ended there, except for the arrival on the field of Benedict Arnold.

Unable to stay back with a battle raging, Arnold mounted his horse and charged into the midst of the fighting. Gates sent a messenger to order him back, but the messenger never caught up with him. Gathering men where he could, Arnold directed an unsuccessful assault on the Balcarres Redoubt. He then turned on the Breymann Redoubt, which fell under his determined attack.[259] Arnold was wounded in this action and unable to follow up his success, but had achieved a decisive penetration of the British defensive line by taking its right flank position. As night fell, the overall strategic situation reached a turning point.

Retreat. During the night of October 7–8 Burgoyne, for the first time, had to pull his own forces back under cover of darkness. He gave up the Balcarres position and consolidated his forces on the high ground around the Great Redoubt. He then took stock of his diminished condition. He had suffered six hundred more casualties during the day and had lost ground. He would finally have to listen to the advice of his subordinates.

The next night Burgoyne again moved, abandoning his fortifications and over five hundred of his sick and wounded. Within a day his army had moved northward to the vicinity of Saratoga. A muster and inventory revealed 3,500 men fit for duty and seven days' provisions on hand.[260]

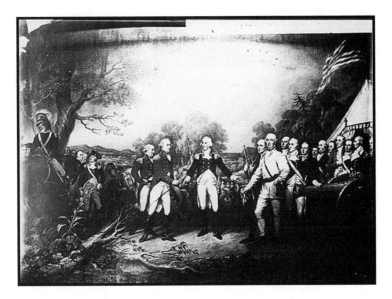

Surrender of General Burgoyne at Saratoga (painting by John Trumbull—National Archives)

SURRENDER

On October 14, 1777, General Burgoyne opened surrender negotiations with General Gates. Gates was well aware of Burgoyne's condition, but also knew that Clinton was having success to the south. Gates totally failed in the art of negotiation. He quickly agreed to all of Burgoyne's demands and revealed his urgency to conclude an agreement. Suspicious of something, Burgoyne delayed for days with the renewed hope that a relief force would save him.

On October 16 a frustrated Gates announced a final deadline and prepared to resume offensive action. Unable to postpone the inevitable any longer, Burgoyne signed the surrender agreement. The next morning his army moved down from the hills around Saratoga to the plains along the Hudson River.

The officers assembled each regiment on parade, inspected their men, and ordered them to ground weapons for the last time. A proud army of British and Hessian regulars ceased to exist as a military entity.

On October 26, Clinton evacuated the captured forts on the Hudson and returned to New York. Within two weeks British forces abandoned Fort Ticonderoga and pulled back into Canada.[261] Washington was no longer trapped between British armies to his north and south. Without a threat from the north, much of Gates's army soon returned to Washington's control. Britain's Grand Strategy had failed.

GOD'S HAND AT SARATOGA

The importance of Burgoyne's surrender at Saratoga cannot be overstated. Most military anthologies include this event as one of the great turning points in history.[262] The effects in America and Europe were dramatic and far-reaching. In America Gates's success was oxygen to a suffocating cause.

General Howe had defeated Washington's army at Brandywine Creek on September 11, and British troops had occupied Philadelphia by the end of the month. The Continental Congress was forced to flee to York and to continue the struggle with an empty treasury and exhausted credit. Morale among the loyalist population was again on the upswing. This dismal picture changed with the uplifting news from Saratoga.

The battles around Freeman's farm and Bemis Heights were especially important to the American army. These actions were not fought behind log revetments, and they were not surprise raids on unprepared defenders. These were intense, stand-up fights in open country against famous British and Hessian front-line regiments. A British officer on the scene observed, "The courage and obstinacy with which the Americans fought were the astonishment of everyone."[263] This performance represented a new aspect of the American war effort.

The most profound effects of the victory were seen in Europe and especially France. The news came to Benjamin Franklin and his fellow commissioners on December 4 and to the French court the next day. Within forty-eight hours Louis XVI and his advisors, abandoning months of indecision, committed France to an alliance with the United States. France signed the long awaited treaty on February 6, 1778, giving the most specific assurance so far that America would ultimately be successful in its war for independence.

Historians have written volumes to apportion the credit and the blame for Saratoga. On the British side there were obvious flaws in planning and coordination, and an underlying arrogance that covered those flaws until it was too late. The Americans showed an unexpected ability to mobilize forces to counter an unexpected threat. Eternal credit goes to the American fighting men who stood the severest test of the war and prevailed against their foe.

Each of these factors was important to the progress of the Saratoga campaign. However, I believe this narrative clearly shows that the outcome was very uncertain even up to the last day. If any one of many small events had played out differently it is not hard to envision Burgoyne reaching Albany in the late summer where units from New York could have supported him logistically. Once in Albany he could have waited for the opportunity to work in cooperation with Howe in a joint campaign. The British war effort would have continued in its ascendancy.

I believe that God moved to ensure that this would not happen. Again, it is in the details that his hand can be seen.

St. Clair's Decision. Military leaders never know when they will face their defining moments. Arthur St. Clair's came on July 5, 1777. He made his decision to abandon Fort Ticonderoga under extreme pressure, but not because of cowardice. He knew that the post had to fall eventually. He had to decide whether or not to sacrifice his men to gain time for the army to the south. He knew that he would be condemned for giving up with so little fight, and in that belief he was correct. He was court-martialed, and, although acquitted, forever lived under the cloud of his actions on that day. I believe that God helped Arthur St. Clair make this difficult but ultimately correct decision, which set the pattern for the entire campaign to come. The Americans would fall back and grow stronger as Burgoyne advanced and grew weaker.

Burgoyne's Delays. Throughout July and August Burgoyne had numerical superiority over the American forces opposing him. The rapid fall of Ticonderoga was an unexpected gift. A decisive breakthrough to Albany was clearly within his grasp. Inexplicably, at this crucial moment, he allowed a lapse in the momentum of his campaign.

Earlier, Burgoyne had weighted his army down with a vast artillery train to make sure that there would be no repeat of Bunker Hill. Like Howe, he learned one lesson too well. Sometimes rapid movement on the battlefield is more decisive than firepower. Burgoyne let a precious month slip away trying to move his army, artillery, and even his own excessive personal baggage over the most difficult route possible from Skenesboro to the Hudson. Moving and resupplying his artillery would be an ongoing drag to British movement during the campaign.

Pride. The proverb says, "Pride goes before destruction."[264] Pride alone accounts for several critical British mistakes. Germain's failure to coordinate and Burgoyne's acquiescence are attributable in some degree to the fact that both men underestimated the capabilities of the colonialists and overestimated British prowess.

Burgoyne's pride ruled in his disastrous choice of a route to the Hudson, leading him to avoid even the appearance of a retreat. I believe that his pride prevented him even considering the option of turning back to Fort Edward on September 13. Regardless of the risk to his army, his own reputation dictated continuing the advance to the south. Again, on October 7, he could not accept the recommendation of his officers to retreat, instead choosing to fight one more battle. At this point Burgoyne might have had to sacrifice his reputation, but he was probably still able to save his army to fight another campaign and to continue the British threat in the north.

In combat, of course, there is often a fine line between reasonable and excessive boldness, and it is always easier to see the difference looking back. However, when we do look back, I believe that we can see God's hand working through John Burgoyne's own pride and ambition.

Breymann's March. If Breymann could have eked out another half mile per hour, he could have prevented the disaster at Bennington. His earlier arrival on the battlefield would have been decisive in not only saving his comrades but also in routing Stark's forces. Breymann's own nature was part of the problem, but would not have been critical with reasonably passable roads. Once again a providential rainstorm turned the tide in an important engagement that would have great bearing on the larger campaign.

The Message. After the first battle at Freeman's farm on September 19 Burgoyne still had parity in troop strength and superiority in military power. The odds for a decisive battle and breakout were still very much in his favor. At this point, the very news that he had waited so long to hear was his undoing. When Clinton's message arrived on September 21, in spite of its ambiguity, Burgoyne relinquished his plan to attack and thereby gave up the initiative of the campaign. His strength would decline over the next several weeks during the time of Gates's most rapid expansion.

Jane McCrea. I do not believe that God caused the death of Jane McCrea. However, I do believe that after this brutal incident occurred, he used it mightily to rouse a population that before then had been extremely slow in responding to a mounting crisis. After this murder in late July, militia ranks throughout New York and New England began to swell. New units arriving in General Gates's camp in early October finally turned the numerical tide against the British and assured the final result.

Chapter Ten
Yorktown

The doctor felt the shock of each earsplitting shot from the big guns. He looked over the vast battlefield. In his years with the army he had never witnessed anything of this magnitude. The allied lines stretched over six miles in a half circle around the fortified British positions along the river below. Relieved briefly from treating his wounded and sick patients, he looked out on the amazing scene. "The bombshells are clearly visible . . . they appear like a fiery meteor with a blazing tail, most beautifully brilliant, ascending majestically from the mortar . . . and gradually descending to the spot where they are destined to execute their work of destruction."[265] Dr. James Thacher had been with units of the Continental Army since the beginning of the war in 1775. He wondered if now, six years later, he might be witnessing the end as he observed the climactic struggle developing around the little village of Yorktown.

AFTER SARATOGA

Burgoyne's surrender at Saratoga brought new life to the anti-war movement in Britain. Agitation against the war swelled as opposition members of Parliament demanded investigations into the debacle. Lord North himself became increasingly uncertain that Britain could win the war. He tried to quell the growing dissent by bringing more members of the opposition into his cabinet and renewing efforts to seek peace in America.

However, in spite of faltering ministers and looming war with France, King George remained implacable. He was committed to defeating the rebellion at whatever the cost and continued to urge his cabinet to firm action. He would countenance no measure conceding power to his foes in Parliament or independence to America. His obstinate stand ensured four more years of war.

The entry of France into the war did have an effect on British strategy. The American colonies became one theater of a larger conflict, as extensive British commercial interests in the Caribbean compelled attention to that area. General Henry Clinton replaced Howe as supreme commander with orders to abandon Philadelphia and to send a portion of his forces to Florida and the Caribbean to defend against anticipated French operations there.

Clinton's headquarters remained in New York where he worked to consolidate an already strong defensive position. A two-year stalemate ensued in the Northern Theater as neither Washington nor Clinton felt strong enough to mount significant offensive operations against the other.

THE SOUTHERN STRATEGY

At this stage of the war the British high command began to focus attention on the southern colonies. A secure base closer to the Caribbean was needed so that forces could be shifted north or south as required. Many believed also that the entire region was less supportive of the rebellion and that a loyalist population would rise up in support of the Crown if given an opportunity. This view persisted in spite of the fact that significant

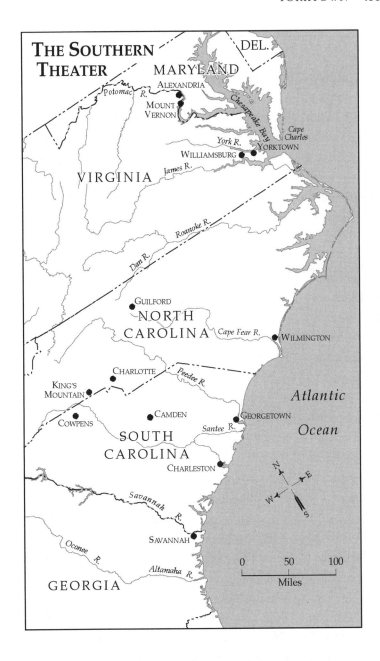

THE SOUTHERN THEATER

DEL.

MARYLAND

ALEXANDRIA

Potomac R.

MOUNT VERNON

Chesapeake Bay

York R.

Cape Charles

YORKTOWN

WILLIAMSBURG

VIRGINIA

James R.

Roanoke R.

Dan R.

GUILFORD

NORTH CAROLINA

Cape Fear R.

WILMINGTON

CHARLOTTE

Peedee R.

KING'S MOUNTAIN

COWPENS

CAMDEN

Santee R.

GEORGETOWN

Atlantic

Ocean

SOUTH CAROLINA

CHARLESTON

N

W — E

S

Savannah R.

SAVANNAH

Oconee R.

Altamaha R.

GEORGIA

0   50   100

Miles

loyalist support for Burgoyne's northern invasion had never materialized.

In July 1779 General Lord Cornwallis arrived in New York to become Clinton's second in command. Cornwallis was an energetic and effective field officer with his own ideas about fighting the war and a strong desire for independent command. His relationship with Clinton would never be smooth. In September 3,800 new troops also arrived in New York, the first reinforcements received in over a year. The stage was finally set for implementation of the southern strategy.

CHARLESTON

In December 1779 Clinton and Cornwallis sailed from New York with a fleet of fourteen warships, ninety transports, and 8,500 men.[266] After a stormy passage these troops were landed on the coast of South Carolina below Charleston and joined forces with other units sent from Georgia and Florida. Clinton then maneuvered his fleet and combined ground force of over thirteen thousand to lay siege to Charleston.

The Continental Congress had earlier commissioned General Benjamin Lincoln to defend South Carolina. With 4,500 troops under his command it was obvious that a defense of Charleston had little chance of success. However, the political pressure on Lincoln to hold the city was intense. He unwisely committed his entire force in the fight for Charleston and in the end suffered the most catastrophic loss of the war. On May 12 he turned over the city and his total force to Clinton in one of the largest surrenders in American military history.[267]

Events moved quickly after the fall of Charleston. Clinton returned to New York with most of his forces, leaving Cornwallis with the independent command that he wanted and the mission to pacify South Carolina and Georgia. Congress sent General Horatio Gates, the public hero of Saratoga, to gather the remnants of the Continental forces in the South to oppose Cornwallis. In one of the most decisive battles of the war, the British completely routed Gates's force at Camden on August 16, 1780.

The American Revolution had suddenly come to its lowest point since December 1776. Except for partisan activity the war in the South seemed to be over. In the North Washington had gone for over a year without men or supplies to mount a significant action. Even though a French force had arrived in Rhode Island, the English fleet had it bottled up in Newport. The Congress was essentially bankrupt, with no funds or credit and a currency that had depreciated to the point of worthlessness.

The Continental Army continued to suffer severe deprivations in food, clothing, medicine, and arms. Desertions were common, and enlistments were dropping. Washington wrote in October, "We have been half our time without provisions and are like to continue so. We have no Magazines, nor money to form them and in a little time we shall have no men (even) if we had money to pay them. We have lived on expedients till we can live no longer."[268]

It would take faithful men and miraculous events to turn the tide in this crisis.

GREENE'S RETREAT

Late in 1780, Congress appointed Nathaniel Greene, one of Washington's most capable and trusted generals, to take over the Southern Department from the discredited Gates. Greene's cautious generalship and Cornwallis's excessive boldness would soon work to change the nature of the war in the South.

General
Lord
Charles
Cornwallis
(painting
by Sir W.
Beechey—
National
Archives)

Greene arrived in Charlotte in early December to take command of about 1,400 demoralized and disorganized troops. At first there was little that he could do to oppose Cornwallis. When he finally received additional troops, he made the rather unusual decision to split his forces, detaching half his men under Brigadier General Daniel Morgan. Morgan was one of the real heroes of Saratoga. Greene thought that his army could subsist better in smaller groups and that he would have more flexibility in reacting to Cornwallis's movements.

Cornwallis's decisive victory at Camden seemed to fire his ambition. Even though his orders from Clinton directed him to maintain a firm hold on South Carolina, Cornwallis had bigger ideas. With reinforcements he felt that he could win the war with a campaign through North Carolina and into Virginia. Clinton effectively lost control of events in the South as Cornwallis obtained approval for his plans directly from Lord Germain in London.

On January 17, 1781, units of Cornwallis's army under Colonel Banastre Tarleton attacked Morgan at Cowpens. In one of the most brilliantly fought engagements of the war, Morgan inflicted a stinging defeat on Tarleton. After the battle, Morgan withdrew to the north and maneuvered to reunite with Greene.

Cornwallis immediately advanced northward in pursuit. He abandoned large amounts of equipment and stores to speed his advance, hoping to bring on a decisive engagement with Greene's army. Greene never let this happen. Keeping in mind his larger mission, he did not allow the British to pin down his army. He fought frequent skirmishes and managed to keep ahead of the British over a two hundred-mile expanse of harsh winter landscape. On February 15 Greene took his forces across the Dan River into Virginia on boats that he had wisely positioned beforehand for that purpose.

At this point Cornwallis finally had to turn his exhausted and hungry army around. He had no supplies, and the hoped-for outburst of loyalist support never seemed to materialize. He conducted his own retreat to Wilmington to resupply and regroup. He had momentarily driven Greene out of North Carolina, but had failed utterly in his own strategic mission. He did not hold South Carolina or defeat Greene's army. He subsequently decided to take his army into Virginia, having forfeited the primary goals of his campaign.

Few commanders become famous for their retreats. However, in this campaign Nathaniel Greene proved himself a great general. He never lost sight of the fact that he would ultimately prevail only if he preserved his army. As Cornwallis turned north, Greene returned to his main task, restoring American control over the South. An important turning point of the war had been reached.

STATE OF THE WAR—1781

In early 1781 the seemingly endless war started into its fifth year. Opposition to the war in England had grown quiet after Lord North's government won a general election in the fall of 1780. The war seemed to be going well enough, especially in the South. There was an appearance of progress, as Cornwallis seemed to advance at will through the Carolinas. On the American side, there was little room for optimism. Even though France had entered the war and French ground and naval units were at Newport, no significant action had so far been possible. The British navy continued to dominate the North American coast and to resupply and reposition forces whenever necessary.

British Command. The dark side of the British war effort was command and control. Even though the chain of command was simple, the key leaders seemed constantly at cross-purposes. In London, Germain seemed to be in a vacuum of his own. Writing to Clinton in December 1780, he stated, "So very contemptible is the rebel force now in all parts, and so vast is our superiority, that no resistance on their part is to be apprehended that can materially obstruct the progress of the King's arms in the speedy suppression of the rebellion."[269] Clinton could only wonder about the source of such a rosy assessment.

Germain assured confusion in authority by dealing directly with Cornwallis when it suited him. Clinton was against Cornwallis's abandonment of South Carolina, but was overridden by Germain. In early 1781, Germain even directed Clinton to make Cornwallis's advance the "principle object for the employment of all forces under your command."[270] Clinton considered his "principle object" to be holding New York and Charleston. As senior commander he was now given the role of reacting to the initiatives of a subordinate.

For his part, Cornwallis departed Wilmington for Virginia in April 1781, without orders from anyone. He somehow had concluded that the war had to be won in Virginia, leaving Nathaniel Greene behind him to threaten a tenuous British infrastructure in the Carolinas. Clinton not only learned of this move belatedly, but Germain then ordered him to support it.

A strange incident occurred to further confuse the British high command. On May 31 Washington wrote a letter to Lafayette in Virginia detailing plans for a combined French and American attack on New York. Due to changing events, this attack never took place. However, when the letter fell into the hands of General Clinton, the results were dramatic.

Clinton's confusion over Washington's intentions and ambivalence toward Cornwallis's campaign produced one of the most bewildering sequence of orders ever issued by a commander. On June 11 he directed Cornwallis to return six battalions of infantry and all possible artillery and cavalry to New York to defend against an expected attack. On June 26, he issued new orders to send these troops to Philadelphia instead of New York. On July 20 he directed Cornwallis to recall all of these troops and to secure a naval base on the Chesapeake.

With considerable chagrin, Cornwallis finally focused on the latter task and selected a site on the York River near its entrance to the bay. He began laying out fortifications at Yorktown and immediately across the river at Gloucester Point. In early August he began assembling all his units into these positions to await the arrival of British naval support and further orders.

American Command. George Washington had command and control problems of his own. General Greene was fighting in the Carolinas and Lafayette was in Virginia with a small force opposing Cornwallis's advance. General Rochambeau remained in Newport, and a French fleet was reported to be somewhere in the Caribbean. It took weeks to get information and to exchange orders and reports. Uncertain lines of authority between the Americans and their new French allies were an even greater concern.

General Comte de Rochambeau (painting by J. D. Court—National Archives)

In a May meeting with Rochambeau, Washington pressed strongly for a consolidation of forces and attack on New York. Rochambeau thought such a move too risky, but was reluctant to publicly disagree with Washington. After agreeing to the plan, he wrote directly to the French naval commander in the Caribbean, requesting that he designate the Chesapeake as the destination for his fleet.[271] This would shift the focus away from New York.

Meanwhile Rochambeau marched his force from Newport overland to join forces with Washington in White Plains. By then Clinton was furiously making defensive preparations, based on the captured letter of May 31. When Washington reached New York, he was able to survey Clinton's defenses in detail and began finally to have second thoughts about his own plan. On August 1 he wrote in his diary, "I could scarce see a ground upon which to continue my preparations against New York."[272] A period of uncertainty settled over the allied armies.

YORKTOWN

Opportunity. The cloud over Washington lifted as Rochambeau's scheme came to fruition. On August 14, 1781, dramatic news arrived. A French frigate slipped into Newport with a dispatch from the French Caribbean fleet. Admiral DeGrasse advised that he was departing the Caribbean with twenty-five to thirty ships and embarked ground forces. His destination was the Chesapeake Bay.

At about the same time Washington received information from Lafayette in Virginia that Cornwallis was moving down the York peninsula toward Portsmouth. Although Washington did not know Cornwallis's intentions, he knew that a long awaited opportunity was presenting itself.

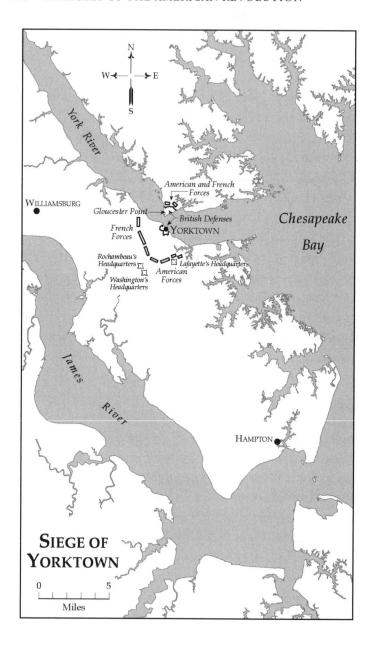

Siege of Yorktown

Reacting quickly, he put half of his army and all of Rochambeau's troops on the march toward Virginia. He detailed the remainder of his forces to deceive the British in New York. Dispatches were sent to Lafayette to expect DeGrasse and to deploy all available troops to prevent Cornwallis's withdrawal. Orders were given to the French naval squadron in Newport, under Admiral DeBarras, to proceed to the Chesapeake.

Battle of the Virginia Capes. Admiral DeGrasse reached the Chesapeake on August 30, debarked his troops and assisted the Americans in repositioning their forces. On September 5, one of his pickets sighted a British fleet outside the entrance to the bay. Aware that DeBarras was coming from Newport and would be vulnerable to this new threat, DeGrasse gave up the safety of his position and sortied into the Atlantic.

The battle of the Virginia Capes ensued between the two fleets, both of which were roughly comparable in strength. After a sharp engagement late in the afternoon, action broke off at nightfall. Each side had inflicted significant damage and casualties on the other, although a decisive result was not achieved. For several days both fleets made repairs and maneuvered for position against each other.

On September 9 DeBarras finally arrived and slipped into the Chesapeake. With thirty-six French ships on the scene, the British fleet withdrew. They had lost the opportunity to aid Cornwallis ashore or to afflict further damage on the French fleet. DeGrasse had masterfully accomplished his strategic mission and had given the American and French forces their first experience of naval superiority in any theater of the war. They would not waste the opportunity.

On to Yorktown. Washington's decision to move the bulk of his army to Virginia had extreme risks. His small force remaining around New York was immediately vulnerable to over seventeen thousand British troops defending the city.[273] The Americans could not hope to contain an offensive move by Clinton into any surrounding area. The rest of Washington's army was equally in jeopardy as it moved carefully around New York. To deceive the British, Washington established a fake encampment in New Jersey to give the appearance of preparations for an attack on Staten Island. To further maintain secrecy, allied leaders did not even inform their men of the true destination. Fortunately, these measures were successful, as Clinton remained in the dark until early September.[274]

By the second week of September Washington's forces reached the northern Chesapeake, where they experienced first-hand the benefits of DeGrasse's successful defense of the Virginia Capes. French naval transports were on hand to save weeks and hundreds of miles of hard marching. After a ferrying operation, the French and Continental troops were ashore at Williamsburg by September 26 and marching on nearby Yorktown.

Washington's combined forces were impressive as the climactic engagement drew near. His own troops joined with those of Lafayette and the Virginia militia to bring the American total to over eight thousand. Combining Rochambeau's army and the units embarked with DeGrasse's fleet, there were over seven thousand French troops.[275] The key to success or failure, however, was the French fleet. As long as it could maintain its presence in nearby waters, there would be a shield against reinforcement, resupply, and even evacuation of Cornwallis's army. If in place, this shield would render the outcome certain.

By late September Clinton was aware of Cornwallis's plight. The British fleet was in port in New York making repairs from the naval battle on September 5. Clinton organized a relief force of seven thousand troops to go to the aid of Cornwallis. Ship

Battle at Yorktown (painting by Turgis—National Archives)

repairs, however, went ahead slowly. In October an English staff officer wrote in his journal, "If the Navy are not a little more active they will not get a sight of the Capes of Virginia before the end of this month, and then it will be a little too late."[276] The relief force in fact was one week too late, as it finally put to sea on October 19.

The Siege. At Yorktown Cornwallis deployed his force of about seven thousand in two defensive rings. His inner position consisted of a series of batteries and redoubts, supported by two ships at anchor offshore. An outer defense line was established about half a mile beyond the inner ring on favorable ground. British forces also occupied Gloucester Point lying about half a mile across the York River from Yorktown.

The American army began to deploy around Yorktown on September 28 in a great arc extending over six miles. On September 30 they were pleasantly surprised to see the British evacuating their outer defensive works. Reduction of these positions would have been costly and time consuming. However, Cornwallis had received a dispatch from Clinton the day before advising him to expect a relief force "in a few days." Cornwallis decided that he would be better able to conserve his forces by concentrating in his inner positions.

In early October the Americans commenced careful and deliberate siege operations. They positioned artillery batteries at key points and then started work on a series of parallel trench lines that moved closer each day to the British positions. An almost constant exchange of artillery fire accompanied this work.

On October 14 American and French infantry assaulted and captured two of the British redoubts. The next night the British counterattacked with their own infantry and temporarily disabled several batteries before being driven off. The trench diggers and artillerymen, however, continued to wage the main battle. The Americans extended their trenches ever closer to the main British position, as the British guns were silenced, one by one.

On the night of October 16 Cornwallis initiated another bold but dangerous move. He decided to conduct a withdrawal of his forces across the York River to Gloucester Point. Washington had accomplished the same feat over a greater distance in his retreat from Long Island. If the British could have crossed the river and penetrated the thin defenses around Gloucester there would have been nothing to impede their progress to the north. All available barges and flatboats were assembled, and the first wave of troops made the crossing around midnight. However, before the boats could return, a gale force wind came up to scatter most of the boats down the river and effectively put a stop to the operation. A New Jersey officer observed that this was "almost as severe a storm as I ever remember to have seen."[277]

Surrender of Lord Cornwallis at Yorktown (painting by John Trumbull—U.S. Capitol Rotunda)

The next morning an officer waving a white flag walked out from the British lines. The siege was over. Many were surprised at the suddenness of the surrender, expecting the campaign to go on for weeks. An American officer remarked, "His surrender was eight or ten days sooner than the most sanguine expected."[278] The British did have ample food and ammunition available to continue the fight. Even though he knew a relief force was coming, Cornwallis decided to wait no longer. On October 19, 1781, he surrendered his command and British hopes for a successful war.

GOD'S PROVIDENTIAL HAND

The Revolutionary War finally came to the South. The fall of Charleston and destruction of Gates's army at Camden were unparalleled disasters. The British invaded North Carolina and southern Virginia in turn. Apathy in this region toward the war was no longer an option.

British success did bring out loyalist sentiment, but this phenomenon did not last. Cornwallis's subordinate, Banastre Tarleton, single-handedly alienated large segments of the population with his brutal reprisals against civilians. Ultimately, Cornwallis's abandonment of his mission to hold the Carolinas left the loyalists who had come to his side completely vulnerable. God's purpose was accomplished, as unity among the colonies grew stronger.

When Cornwallis quit the Carolinas and Greene turned to his own mission, another great purpose was achieved. If peace had come while a British infrastructure was in place in North Carolina, South Carolina, and Georgia, this region would probably have remained part of the British Empire. Under the legal concept known as *uti possidetis* belligerents retain the territory actually occupied at the time of a cessation in hostilities.[279] Thanks to Cornwallis's failure and Greene's success, this did not happen to the South. This region would become an integral component of the new nation.

Political cohesiveness progressed a long way during these final years of the war. Political, diplomatic, and military leaders established reputations that would be vital to the unity and success of the new nation. A continuing government was finally assured in March 1781 when Maryland became the last state to ratify the Articles of Confederation. Maryland had held out because of a dispute over land claims to the western territories. Virginia finally relinquished its claim to the Ohio lands as a gesture of compromise, but only as British troops were invading. Amazingly, at this critical turn, the war took precedence over rival economic interests and brought a new degree of unity to the new nation.[280]

Apparently when the British invaded the South in 1781, God's timetable was ready for the beginning of the end to the American Revolution. This can be seen in retrospect, although it was not obvious then. The outcome continued to be highly uncertain. The surrender of another great British army was unimaginable at that time. Such a debacle should have been impossible considering the combined strength of British ground and naval forces available to prevent it. Only a combination of the most amazing events of the war could have brought about the great climax.

British Confusion. Lapses in vision and judgment on the part of British leaders have been a recurring theme of this book. During the Yorktown campaign, the lack of cooperation among the three principle British leaders was so complete as to be miraculous in itself. Germain had shown his incompetence earlier in the war, as detailed in chapters five and six, and can certainly be blamed for the basic problem in command relationships during this campaign. Clinton and Cornwallis, however, were both capable officers who had shown great initiative and skill throughout their careers. For them to continue at cross-purposes to the point of losing an army is inexplicable.

The Mysterious Letter. Henry Clinton had shown himself to be a decisive officer on numerous occasions. It was uncharacteristic of him to be nervous, especially while occupying a strong defensive position such as that at New York during this period. Still he kept a wary eye on Rochambeau in Newport and Washington along the Hudson. When Washington's uncoded, handwritten letter of May 31 fell into his hands, he seemed to have irrefutable evidence of his enemy's intentions. Unfortunately for Clinton, Washington's intentions were changed by events. Working on this apparently reliable information, Clinton proceeded to hopelessly confuse Cornwallis with contradicting orders. He then completely missed the main thrust of Washington's army to the south and passed up a golden opportunity to strike Washington while on the move.

Storm at Gloucester Point. Washington's nighttime evacuation of Long Island in 1776 was blessed with perfect weather conditions that changed for his benefit at almost precise moments. Cornwallis had no such "luck." Gale force winds at the worst possible moment completely disrupted his last chance for evacuation.

Fateful Decisions. Cornwallis's situation was not hopeless up until the moment that he raised the white flag. A relief force was on the way. Unfortunately, Clinton did not have the sense of urgency that was called for in this situation. He could have gotten there sooner. Also, his message to Cornwallis to expect support within a few days dangerously misled his beleaguered compatriot. In retrospect, Cornwallis's decision to abandon his outer defenses cost him the time that might have produced his salvation. On the other hand Cornwallis could have also bought time by holding out longer. He had the supplies and the position. Amazingly, at that moment, he lost the will.

The Main Miracle. It is difficult to appreciate command and control problems in an era of courier-delivered mail between units dispersed over thousands of miles. Plans and orders might be based on information weeks or months old and then be weeks or months in transit to the subordinate command concerned. Compared to the American/French problems in coordination, the British had the advantage of a fairly simple command structure. Washington had to rely on the uncertain support of his own political superiors and the cooperation of French army and naval commanders with unclear lines of authority.

In dealing with all of these problems Washington had been extremely "fortunate" in being able to keep the war going for over five years while avoiding a catastrophic defeat. However, he had found it impossible to focus enough land and naval forces at any point to inflict a decisive defeat on his foe. Keenly aware throughout the war of his vulnerability to British sea power, he knew that this aspect of the war was critical to the success of any strategy that he might devise. The arrival of the French fleet in the Chesapeake presented a fleeting opportunity.

There were many good decisions made by Washington and the French commanders leading to success at the Virginia Capes and Yorktown. Historians have justly recognized them for the brilliance of this campaign. Only when we consider the intricacy of these events and the precise coordination of forces over vast distances do we see the miraculous nature of this victory and the hand of God at work. In *Sea Power*, the authors state:

> Miracles do not often occur in military and naval operations, but Yorktown was a miracle. At a time when the American cause was disintegrating, it brought victory. At a time when the British could not effectively coordinate two armies in the colonies . . . it was an example of perfect coordination of a fleet with the armies of two different nations. At a time when communications were slow and unreliable, it demonstrated precise timing on the part of forces 1,500 miles apart.[281]

The coauthor of this widely used naval text was Chester Nimitz, the commander of United States naval forces in the Pacific theater in World War II. He was well acquainted with miraculous naval operations from his firsthand experience at the Battle of Midway on June 4, 1942.

PART FOUR

THE MIRACLES

CHAPTER ELEVEN
ANOTHER PERSPECTIVE

"America in her revolution proclaimed the wider rights of mankind. Across the Atlantic shone a noble example of freedom which in the end was to exercise a formidable influence upon the world. But in the eighteenth century America's commanding future was scarcely foreseen, even by her own statesmen."

—WINSTON CHURCHILL[282]

TODAY, WE CAN see the American Revolution as one of the great events in human history. However, from the perspective of Europe during the eighteenth and nineteenth centuries, a revolt of colonists in the new world was of somewhat minor importance. For centuries the great European powers were in a constant state of competition on the continent and around the globe for trade and territory. These countries combined into shifting alliances and fought frequent wars, as their professional military forces clashed in great battles on land and sea. At the time, a conflict between one of these powers and her colonies, though unusual, was secondary to the main events of the time.

GREAT BRITAIN

For many years the people of Great Britain had difficulty comprehending that there was even a problem in America. Large numbers of Englishmen went to North America to establish permanent settlements, as opposed to many Europeans who went to the New World seeking to bring home its natural resources. Britain's colonies flourished as their populations and commerce expanded, to the benefit of both colonies and mother country.

Britain's primary enemy for over a century was France. A very unfriendly competition developed between the two countries for power, commerce, and territory. Between 1689 and 1815 they fought seven wars. France usually concentrated her resources on her army, having to face other foes on the continent. Britain, on the other hand, was primarily a trading nation and relied on a powerful navy to protect her homeland and commercial empire abroad. The success of that naval strategy added Nova Scotia, Newfoundland, the Hudson Bay territory, Gibraltar, and Minorca to the empire during the early 1700s.[283]

During the Seven Years' War Britain achieved even more astounding results. Under the leadership of William Pitt, Britain continued to avoid serious engagement on the continent and fought a highly successful naval and amphibious war specifically designed to further expand her trading empire. She established control over India, Canada, and all territory in North America east of the Mississippi, including Florida. In 1763 Britain stood as the dominant nation in the world.

Two decades later this mighty military power was unaccountably defeated by an ad hoc army of rebellious colonists and forces supplied by their own former enemy, France. To the astonishment of the world, Britain lost two entire armies to surrender in the field, and her navy suffered one of its few defeats in a century. This book has detailed the miraculous circumstances that came together during this brief span leading to Britain's loss of her North American colonies.

After the American Revolution, Britain continued to war with France, almost without pause, for another thirty years. In sharp contrast to the period of American conflict, stable government was reestablished by the son of William Pitt. The "Younger" Pitt was called to lead the cabinet in 1783 and held power for almost twenty years. With steady civilian direction and the leadership of Admiral Horatio Nelson, the British navy resumed its dominance and eradicated French naval power at Trafalgar. The Duke of Wellington led an allied army that confronted and defeated Napoleon at Waterloo. British supremacy continued after the astounding but brief debacle in America.

FRANCE

The Seven Years' War devastated France. At once she saw her colonial empire fragmented and her financial condition drastically weakened. A long and difficult rebuilding process followed during the next two decades as resentment toward the British smoldered.

At first, the French took mild comfort in Britain's problems with her colonies in North America. They could feel good that their old adversary had new problems, even though they were ambivalent about becoming involved. Military weakness made open conflict out of the question. The French government could provide clandestine support to the colonists up to a certain level, but the king was reluctant to do too much that would encourage open revolt against another monarch.

Gradually, the French role in America deepened. There was widespread popular support for the Americans, who seemed to be successfully putting the ideals of France's own Enlightenment into practice. The American diplomats, particularly Benjamin Franklin, became popular heroes and effective lobbyists for the colonists' cause.

The British surrender at Saratoga in 1777 was a turning point. This military victory established the viability of the young United States and motivated the French government to move directly to a military alliance. By that time the French military establishment was ready for action. War on the side of America seemed to present a good opportunity to redress past wrongs.

France's overt entry into the war broadened its scale, but produced no immediate results. To George Washington's great disappointment, the first French fleet deployed under Admiral Charles le Comte d'Estaing accomplished little in Caribbean or American waters for over a year. D'Estaing returned to France, severely wounded, after a poorly coordinated and unsuccessful attack on Savannah in October 1779. In 1780 another fleet with an embarked army under General Rochambeau came to America. However, British ships succeeded in blockading these forces in Newport. Meanwhile, the British retained the initiative by taking Charleston and invading the Carolinas, as the war reached one of its lowest points for the Americans and the French.

This dismal picture changed suddenly with the miraculous events at the Virginia Capes and Yorktown, explained in chapter ten. Somehow, for a few days the British lost naval superiority at the scene of a major battle for the only time in the war. Admiral DeGrasse arrived at the perfect time and place and maneuvered his fleet flawlessly to accomplish this feat.

In contrast to this great victory, DeGrasse was decisively defeated a few months later in the Caribbean. During the battle of the Saints on April 12, 1782, a British fleet scattered his own and forced him to surrender his ruined flagship. One of the great heroes of the American Revolution eventually returned to France in disgrace.

France received little for her efforts in the war. The peace treaty restored her African possessions and a few Caribbean islands. Except for Yorktown, however, she was unable to inflict a decisive military defeat on her old enemy or to occupy new territory. She had the pale satisfaction of seeing Britain lose her North American colonies but not much else. Unfortunately, France's most direct reward for her effort was a catastrophic increase in her national debt.

THE FRENCH REVOLUTION

Within a few years the great French Revolution exploded across Europe. Ironically, the inspiration of the American Revolution and France's deteriorating financial condition from supporting it were important factors contributing directly to this upheaval.[284] By 1785 the French government had exhausted its credit.[285] In 1789, when all other measures to restore the economy failed, the French king was forced to call the first national assembly in 175 years. That year and event mark the beginning of the French Revolution. Almost at the precise moment, the first American government elected under its newly ratified Constitution took office. Historians generally consider that this event marked the end of the American Revolution.

The American and French Revolutions were connected in other ways besides time. The ideological climate wrought by the French Enlightenment was fundamental to both. Chapter two explained the effect of Enlightenment thought on the American founders. In turn, the Americans' success in throwing off oppression directly inspired many in France to apply their intellectual heritage to their own national condition. Freedom from tyranny became an attainable goal for Frenchmen.

A sharp contrast between the revolutions existed, however, in the area of religion. The religious climate in America during its revolutionary period has been a focus of this book. The underlying situation in France was, of course, very different. The Catholic Church was the official state church of France. The church was powerful and rich, owning about one-fifth of the land in France and all the income from it.[286] The combined power of church and state had contained the spiritual challenge of the Reformation. French Huguenot history included centuries of discrimination, persecution, and exile.

This church power was one of the first targets of the French Revolution. The Civil Constitution of the Clergy was enacted in 1790, providing for confiscation of church property and elimination of compulsory church tithes. This legislation also required clergymen to swear allegiance to France and the Constitution in an attempt to sever ties to the Roman church.[287]

The attack on the church went far beyond structural issues, however, and eventually focused on religion itself. In the tradition of the Enlightenment, reason was elevated and extolled, as faith was attacked and discredited. During 1792 and 1793 the country went through an intense period of de-christianization, described by one historian in these words:

> Priests were compelled to abjure their vocation; there was sacrilegious masquerading, vandalism, and destruction of churches; a new calendar was enforced, which got rid of Sundays and Saints' days. In the end a revolutionary religion was introduced to serve the moral ends of the nation in place of discredited Catholicism.[288]

This frenzied activity reached its peak on November 10, 1793, as the Festival of Reason was celebrated in Paris and in many other cities throughout France. At least half of the National Convention delegates went to the cathedral of Notre Dame, redecorated as the Temple of Reason. There they witnessed a Greco-Roman structure built in the church nave that depicted the goddess of Liberty bowing to the flame of Reason.[289]

I would not attempt to discern God's attitude toward these events. An explanation of the French Revolution is beyond the scope of this book and my expertise. Perhaps God's purpose at this time was simply to redress abuses of the Catholic Church in France by drastically curtailing its temporal power. If this was his purpose, he accomplished it completely. It is difficult to speculate about reasons for everything else that occurred during this great upheaval.

It is clear, however, that very few men or women of faith were in control of the French Revolution or the governments that it produced. I cannot prove cause and effect between this fact and the Reign of Terror or subsequent French history. However, people guided purely by reason unleashed the chaos in France that devastated the nation and embroiled all of Europe in war. For years there seemed to be no leaders or political institutions capable of bringing antagonistic factions together. I believe that this history shows the result of human effort without God's providential hand.

The one man who did finally bring France together for a time was Napoleon Bonaparte, one of the great military and civic geniuses of history. His contributions to French glory are legend, and he is now literally enshrined in the memory of France. This was the man who crowned himself king by virtue of his power as commander of the French army. He never gave up that power until he and France were finally and completely defeated on the battlefield. It is interesting to speculate about a Napoleon rising to prominence during the American Revolution. The survival of American democracy under such a man would be difficult to imagine.

Napoleon Bonaparte and George Washington were both military and national leaders during chaotic times of revolution. They present, however, one of history's most stark contrasts. Washington is perhaps a pale comparison to the more dynamic and controversial figure of Napoleon. However, he possessed one startling trait of character that Napoleon lacked. He was blessed with a humility that constrained his own ego and allowed him to walk away from power for the sake of a higher purpose than himself. In the principled leadership of this man through America's most difficult years, I believe we do see a history affected by God's providential hand.

Chapter Twelve
Miracles of the Revolution

"Liberty regards religion as its companion in all its battles and its triumphs, as the cradle of its infancy and the divine source of its claims. It considers religion as the safeguard of morality, and morality as the best security of law and the surest pledge of the duration of freedom.

Religion in America takes no direct part in the government of society, but it must be regarded as the first of their political institutions; for if it does not impart a taste for freedom, it facilitates the use of it."

—ALEXIS DE TOCQUEVILLE[290]

D E TOCQUEVILLE was a French historian who traveled throughout America in the 1830s seeking to understand how a new nation could be so successful. He published his findings in two volumes that offer a unique, outsider's perspective of the founding and early development of the dynamic young republic. His goal was to discover the source of America's greatness and to explain this phenomenon to Europeans of that era.

America continues to be a great nation today. In many respects it is the greatest nation in history. Less than two hundred years after its founding, it emerged as one of the world's pre-eminent powers. Since the collapse of the Soviet Union in 1991, America has stood alone as the world's single superpower. The level of technological innovation, wealth creation, economic security, and military power seen in America today has never before existed.

Most Americans today give little thought to how or why this condition has come about. To most, historical events in retrospect seem to have just happened through a random and ill-defined process. If asked specifically, many would credit America's greatness to its stable government or its abundant natural resources. Considering the same explanation, De Tocqueville observed, "In what portion of the globe shall we find more fertile plains, mightier rivers, or more unexplored and inexhaustible riches than South America? Yet South America has been unable to maintain democratic institutions."[291]

De Tocqueville searched for the greatness of America in her harbors, rivers, fertile fields, forests, mines, vast commerce, democratic government, and "matchless constitution." To some extent he found answers in all of these areas. However, he often came back to a more basic advantage: "There is no country in the world where the Christian religion retains a greater influence over the souls of men than in America; and there can be no greater proof of its utility and of its conformity to human nature than that its influence is powerfully felt over the most enlightened and free nation of the earth."[292]

I also believe in America's greatness. I have sought to discover the source of this greatness by seeking to better understand how and why America came to exist. The approach of this book has been to look deeply into the men and events surrounding America's founding and to search the complexity of this history for an understanding of God's purpose and influence. I believe that the historical facts demonstrate clearly that America's founding was not a lucky or random phenomenon, but instead reveal God's hand in a great and pivotal historical event.

THE AMERICAN REVOLUTION

This story began with the British Empire at the peak of its power following an overwhelming victory in the Seven Years' War. Britain's position in North America was stronger than ever, supported by an underlying gratitude and loyalty among the colonists themselves. I believe that we can see God working to change this picture through an intricate series of events.

To begin with, a young, inexperienced, and somewhat neurotic prince came to the British throne at a particularly inopportune time due to the unexpected deaths of his father and grandfather. The new king then surrounded himself with a series of exceptionally shortsighted and inept ministers. Constant turnover within the cabinet served to further aggravate this condition.

William Pitt was the one proven statesman in British politics, but the king personally disliked him and pointedly shunned him for years. When Pitt was finally called to serve, sickness and a bizarre case of medical malpractice combined to stop him from implementing his plans. For two decades the king and his ministers seemed incapable of grasping Britain's own long-term interest. They took one disastrous step after another toward alienating and losing their prized possession and hope for the future, the North American colonies.

During these same decades another group of leaders gradually took shape in America. These men were from different backgrounds and brought their own biases, ambitions, and imperfections to an ill-defined task. They also brought together the most remarkable collection of political talent and leadership ability ever seen at one time and place. They were blessed with the propensity to work together in support of a great cause. This group of men represents one of the most tangible manifestations of God's presence in history. These men, often giving credit themselves to God, were instrumental in articulating the colonial cause against Great Britain, organizing peaceful protest and armed resistance, and bringing about independence. They fought a full-scale war, and laid the foundation of the most successful form of government ever created, including provisions for its future expansion and continuing renewal. From this group of men, leaders then stepped forward to guide the new nation during its most vulnerable early years.

Of all the founders, George Washington was the central figure in this story. His early military career was not distinguished, and his appointment to lead the Continental Army was a political compromise. Nevertheless he proved to be one of the great generals in history.

The most miraculous aspect of Washington's life is the fact that he was never captured, wounded, or killed on the battlefield. Incidents in Braddock's campaign, Long Island, Trenton, Princeton, and Brandywine have all been documented. There were also frequent plots to usurp his position, and he was vulnerable to such threats at many low points in the war. His survival and continuity in command were vital to the war effort and to his subsequent standing as a venerated military and political figure.

Washington's person and reputation gave legitimacy to the Constitution and office of the presidency. His prestige held a fractious nation together through its most trying years. A man of less moral fiber in his position could easily have made himself a military dictator, permanent president, or even king. Instead, time after time he relinquished his power for the benefit of the nation. Time after time he also called his countrymen back to God, the source of his own strength and the true architect of America's founding.

GOD'S PURPOSE

As a Christian I believe strongly that God has a purpose for individual human beings. He wants each to enjoy a relationship with him, in this life and in the eternal future. He has also provided the way for this to happen. His son, Jesus Christ, came into the world to overcome the barriers separating humanity from God. Every other religion requires that men and women work their way to God through various processes of self-improvement or even self-perfection. Christ requires only that we accept God's gift. To do this, each individual has to make a decision.

For his own reasons, God gave human beings the free will to make this decision as well as every other choice in life. Every person is free to seek God or to turn away from him, each according to his or her own conscience. Without this freedom, faith in God would be a meaningless concept. People can work out God's plan for themselves only when they can make these spiritual choices without coercion.

I believe that God's purpose for America is directly related to his underlying purpose for individual men and women. Human freedom and the exercise of free will are necessary for people to seek God in the only meaningful way possible, personally and freely. Unfortunately, free societies have not been common in history, and, as pointed out by John Witherspoon, religious freedom has seldom survived without civil liberty. The Founding Fathers institutionalized both civil and religious freedom in America, and I believe that this embodied the essence of God's purpose for America.

GOD AND WAR

In considering God's actions in history, the subject of war has to be addressed. The idea that God would cause war is difficult to imagine. I do not think that this happens. Human beings themselves are the source of most conflict in the world, whether at the interpersonal or international level. I believe that God is disappointed when such conflict occurs. However, I also believe that there is no human situation that God cannot use to fulfill his own purpose.

Armed conflict between Britain and her North American colonies was not inevitable. For years the colonial leaders voiced their complaints respectfully, with a deeply held conviction that they themselves were Englishmen. For years they sought simply to have their grievances redressed so that normal life and commerce could resume. If the British king or Parliament had taken a broader view of these issues, this should have happened. Some peaceful solution was in the overwhelming best interest of Britain. At the time it was also in the perceived interest of practically every colonial leader to avoid an open conflict.

We like to think that reasonable men should be able to settle differences without violence. Most of the time this is true, and this could have been the case in America before 1775. Unfortunately, a new and insecure king, a Parliament and ministers with narrow vision, and colonialists with a growing frustration level finally produced the violence that practically no one wanted. By the time shots were fired at Lexington on April 19, 1775, war had become inevitable.

At several points I have drawn parallels between the American Revolution and the biblical story of the Israelites' exodus from Egypt. In this story God was the central figure, working on many levels. His plan was to bring freedom to an enslaved people and to make those people into a nation. To accomplish his purpose he worked through great and small men with all their inherent strengths and weaknesses, and he also performed miracles.

God did not make freedom and nationhood an easy process for the Israelites. At times he actually seemed to create obstacles himself. Scripture relates that he repeatedly "hardened the heart" of Pharaoh, ensuring that the conflict would become even more intense.[293] Then, what should have been a ten-day trek to the so-called Promised Land became a journey of forty years' duration. Time after time these people came to the end of their resources and to the point where there was nothing left but to rely on God. Time after time God worked miracles to sustain the Israelites and to demonstrate his own nature to them. Through all of this time of shared hardship, sacrifice, and danger, a new nation was formed.

At the time of the American Revolution many religious leaders believed that America was the new Israel, brought forth by God to be a light of freedom to the rest of the world. America's own exodus involved a long war and years of sacrifice and hardship. Freedom did not come easily to America either. Many of the founders themselves saw God's miracles working to sustain a cause frequently on the verge of extinction. The path to nationhood was also difficult, as it had to be. Unity came slowly and painfully over a period of years as the war touched one region after another. The evidence of God's hand in America's exodus is plainly visible today in the historical record presented in part three.

GOD'S HAND IN THE REVOLUTIONARY WAR

On June 17, 1775, the rebellion in America should have ended before it had a chance to begin. If John Stark and his New Hampshire men had not arrived on the scene that afternoon, and if Stark had ignored the beach along the Mystic River, the battle of Bunker Hill would have been over in minutes. Howe's first attack would have bypassed and cut off Prescott's men in the main redoubt on top of the hill. It is not hard to imagine the victorious British units quickly completing the rout of the remaining rebel forces around Boston. The same result is likely to have occurred if Howe's artillerymen had brought the proper cannonballs to the battle, or if navy ships had deployed up the Mystic River as requested. The British did finally "win" the battle, but at an extremely heavy cost. Even though the Americans themselves thought they were beaten, the British commanders were stunned by the results of their victory. For the remainder of the war the British generals that saw this action were excessively cautious about attacking rebel defensive works.

For nine months British forces sat idly in Boston, ignoring all evidence that the Americans were on the verge of disintegration. Any bold action by the British during these many months probably would have brought a swift end to the insurrection. Unaccountably, Dorchester Heights, the key terrain dominating the city and harbor, remained unnoticed and unoccupied. On March 4, 1776, Washington was finally able to take the initiative with a risky nighttime move onto those heights. Without perfect weather conditions during the night, a very unusual storm the next day, and ignored warnings by the British, Washington would have stepped into a disaster. Instead, the British unexpectedly evacuated Boston. This caused a celebration throughout the colonies at the very moment of stalemate within the Continental Congress over the question of separating from Britain. As a direct result of the amazing victory at Boston, the climactic debate leading to the Declaration of Independence began.

Washington's army marched to New York during the summer of 1776 with a new confidence. After Howe's precipitous evacuation of Boston, there was an optimistic feeling that further armed conflict might not be necessary. These hopes were dispelled when the largest military force ever deployed outside Britain arrived in New York Bay and began to land on Long Island. In a brilliant tactical maneuver, Howe enveloped and crushed Washington's entire forward defensive line on August 27. Again, a determined push by the British should have ended the war that day. This did not happen due to Howe's lack of resolve and miraculous turns in the weather. Northeast winds and heavy rain slowed Howe's advance for days and kept his ships out of the East River where they could have interdicted the American position from the rear. In the midst of Washington's desperate nighttime retreat, the storm ceased at the exact time that his staff concluded that the river crossing was impossible. Then, at first light the next morning, an unusual fog came up over the East River to screen many of Washington's forces still vulnerable in small boats. God's hand seemed to protect the Continental Army from a catastrophic and war-ending defeat, as hardening British attitudes ensured that the war would continue.

By late 1776 it seemed that the war was about over as British and Hessian forces consolidated their hold over all of New York and New Jersey. The Continental Congress had to flee Philadelphia due to the apparent total defeat of Washington's army. The Revolution had come to its darkest hour. In a desperate attempt to turn the tide, Washington risked the remnant of his small army in a night river crossing and attack on the Hessian garrison at Trenton. Unknown to Washington, the Hessians knew that he was coming. Miraculously, a phantom attack and an unopened warning note preserved the secrecy of his true attack and ensured its success. A few days later the weather played another decisive role. Washington, with his back to the Delaware River, faced an unexpectedly swift advance by a superior British force. An unusually warm day on January 2 mired the British advance in mud. A sudden freeze that night enabled Washington's swift movement and surprise attack on Princeton. These small battles changed the course of the war drastically and brought new life to a dying cause.

Burgoyne's attack from Canada in 1777 was a well-designed campaign to split the colonies and end the war. It came agonizingly close to success. At about the same time Washington suffered a defeat in an unsuccessful attempt to defend Philadelphia. A British army at Albany would have put Washington in a hopeless position. This should have and almost did happen. Only an amazing combination of events prevented it. Burgoyne's own faults played a major role, even though he had previously proven himself a capable and aggressive general. His decision to waste weeks thrashing cross-country to the Hudson remains a mystery. When he should have and could have advanced boldly, he seemed to countenance delay after delay. Near the end when he should have used caution to save his army, he pushed blindly ahead. Pride truly seems to have been his downfall. Another blow to Burgoyne's chances came when impassable roads prevented his reinforcements reaching the battlefield at Bennington. The Jane McCrea affair deprived Burgoyne of his Indian scouts at the crucial point of his campaign and became a rallying cry for the militia buildup that would prove decisive at the end. The surrender of Burgoyne's army was one of the pivotal events in history, sending shock waves throughout Europe and America. This American success led directly to French recognition and assistance in the war effort.

The most amazing and miraculous event of the Revolutionary War was the success of the combined American and French forces at Yorktown. It is difficult to summarize all the things that had to fall into place perfectly over a period of months to produce this outcome. On the British side we have Cornwallis's abandonment of the Carolinas, his uncoordinated advance into Virginia, and continued confusion within the British high command. Contrasted to this was the near perfect coordination of the French and American forces on land and sea over distances of thousands of miles. It was actually beyond human ability to intentionally coordinate the intricate timing of all these events. Two French fleets and a British fleet arrived off the Virginia Capes in perfect sequence to enable a French naval victory. For a brief period the allies achieved naval superiority for the first and only time of the war. Even French deception worked to the advantage of the allies, misleading Washington, while hopelessly confusing the British at the most critical moment. Although the allied forces eventually besieged Cornwallis at Yorktown, the outcome was not certain until a sudden and violent storm disrupted his final effort to retreat across the York River. Cornwallis gave up the fight after this setback even though a relief effort was under way and supplies were on hand to continue the struggle. Surrender of another army was the final blow to the British war effort.

The skeptic may be unconvinced by my interpretation of these events. The miracles that I have cited can be viewed as natural phenomena. Taken in isolation, each incident does have some logical explanation. Taken as a whole, however, there is a convincing case that something other than human skill or luck orchestrated the extraordinary sequence of military engagements that led to victory for America in its war of revolution.

RELIGIOUS FREEDOM

Parts one and two of this book show the complex pattern of men and ideas that came together at the founding to establish the relationship between religion and government in the new nation.

The founders were influenced by their knowledge of church history in Europe and the colonies, their own attitudes toward religion, and by the revolutionary crisis of which they were part.

The founders presented in part two were a group of uniquely educated and gifted men, and each was deeply religious in his own way. Each came from a Christian background. Several, including Adams, Franklin, and Madison, had early aspirations to the ministry, and Witherspoon was a practicing minister all his life. They were all affected to some degree by the flowering of religious fervor associated with the Great Awakening. Madison and Witherspoon had a direct connection to this phenomenon through the school founded as a direct outgrowth of it, the College of New Jersey at Princeton. Jefferson may have been the least religious of the founders, but was, throughout his life, deeply devoted to his own search for spiritual truth.

The Enlightenment also had a profound effect on every one of these men. Each founder seemed to respond to the modern importance of reason and scientific knowledge. Jefferson, Madison, and Witherspoon especially were steeped in the latest European philosophical thought as a result of their educational experiences. Although most of the founders saw no conflict between reason and their own religious faith, there was an impact on their individual attitudes toward the religious establishments of the time. Every founder seemed to identify with the attitude that religion should not interfere with scientific inquiry.

Somehow these men and their various approaches to religion were brought together in the formation of America's new government. I believe that John Witherspoon was the key to this achievement. He was a deeply religious man himself, and he believed that the freedom to seek God individually was the foundational freedom of all others. He planted the seed that religious and civil liberty were mutually supporting and equally necessary.

James Madison took these ideas directly to the Virginia legislature, where he and Jefferson formed the mold setting the relationship between religion and government in America. The other founders played their own unique roles in the adoption of this pattern at the national level. We can see in these events that the outcome was not certain. Many at the time would have been happy with an established church on the pattern of the Old World. This was not God's plan.

In its final form the First Amendment to the Constitution was written to provide that "Congress shall make no law respecting an establishment of religion, or prohibiting the free exercise thereof." This historic and carefully wrought phrase served to prevent the federal government establishing an official religion or interfering with the religious practices of its citizens. The United States was the first nation founded on this guarantee. The religious establishment would play no role in government, to the benefit of religion and government. A more rational approach to government would be possible, as well as a more spiritual approach to religion.

In the 1940s, through a series of still controversial decisions connected to the Fourteenth Amendment, the Supreme Court applied the First Amendment to the *states* as well as the federal government. Since then, the courts have been asked to define what constitutes a religion and to interpret which religious practices are protected and which are not. The subsequent legal history of religious freedom in America has been torturous and often dismaying to Christians. Somehow the courts have interpreted the Constitution as requiring an almost complete wall between any level of government and anything religious.

As Americans more and more assume a freedom *from* religion, it is useful to recall how central God was to the lives of the founders and to the new nation. Christianity strongly influenced all of these men, and each was deeply religious in his own way. At the time, almost everyone in the new nation assumed that no religious establishment meant that there would be no established *denomination* of the church. Christianity and God were then at the center of the nation's life.

As the founders severed ties with England and traditional royalty, they considered God to be the source of legitimacy and authority in the new government. On July 4, 1776, Samuel Adams proclaimed, "We have this day restored the Sovereign, to Whom alone men ought to be obedient."[294] All acknowledged that God alone endowed human beings with dignity and inalienable rights and provided the new nation with the foundation of its morality. John Adams asserted, "Our constitution was made for a moral and religious people. It is wholly inadequate for the government of any other."[295] God was central to the American Revolution, and later controversies should not obscure the remarkable nature of what our forefathers achieved and what has continued to prevail: the freedom of every individual to make his or her own decision about God.

RELIGIOUS ESTABLISHMENT

At several points in this book, I have recounted criticisms of the established Christian churches at the time of the Revolution. These criticisms were founded on well-justified fears of ecclesiastical and civil power, especially as they had combined in Europe before the eighteenth century. Most at the time knew about the evils of inquisitions, witch hunts, and the persecution of famous scientists by officials of the church. Clearly, many Christians and church leaders of that era had lost touch with their essential purpose. Unfortunately, many others, in their concern over the structure of the church, also lost the benefit of the message of the church.

Still, we need to remember that there were many who were faithful to the true role of the church over the centuries. The early churches assembled and sanctioned the Bible itself and preserved the essentials of the Christian faith. They spread the gospel around the world and faithfully ministered to millions, both physically and spiritually. Throughout the history of the church, many Christians have worked quietly and humbly to do God's work in the world with no sanction of governmental authority.

Christianity and its many churches were important to Americans at the time of the Revolution. Amazingly, the overthrow of the established civil and ecclesiastical authority in the American colonies was accomplished without violence or even malice toward the churches themselves, in sharp contrast to the European revolutions to follow. Many at the time, especially Christians, were afraid that the disestablished churches would be fatally weakened. Amazingly, this did not happen. The churches emerged with a newfound vitality and in a stronger condition than ever. There was even a Second Great Awakening in the early 1800s, with another surge of Christian spirituality throughout the new nation. Even though no government-sanctioned church establishment survived the Revolution, Christianity continued to be vitally important to the people of the United States.

CHAPTER THIRTEEN
A NEW CALL TO FREEDOM

"America is great because she is good, and if America ever ceases to be good, she will cease to be great."

—ALEXIS DE TOCQUEVILLE[296]

AMERICA AT WAR

For over two hundred years God has continued to bless America with freedom, stable government, and unparalleled prosperity. His providential hand has been especially evident at those critical moments in wartime when the nation's existence has been in jeopardy, from the Revolution to modern times.[297] Unfortunately, conflict in the world continues, and America is not immune to it or isolated from it.

On September 11, 2001, a group of fanatics declared war on America and the rest of the free world. Since then, America has fought the War on Terrorism in Afghanistan, Iraq, and other parts of the world. This conflict also continues in America and has given birth to a new and growing security infrastructure. Americans are paying the human and economic costs of this war and are also suffering encroachments on their freedom due to ever more inconvenient and even abrasive security measures.

Today, more than ever, Americans have difficulty with the idea of war and "enemies." Organized hatred and wars of religion are especially bewildering subjects to most who live in modern Western society. In fact even the term *evil* itself has fallen into disfavor within our culture, as few are comfortable with giving anyone or anything that label. Yet, people continue to perform acts that are unthinking, unjust, and cruel.

Sometimes there are underlying causes, and sometimes there are not. Evil in the world seems very real when we are confronted with the incredible nature of random terrorist attacks on unsuspecting and defenseless people.

It is my belief that ultimately God will not favor any group that employs purposeful violence against innocent people and especially those who try to preempt their religion for a political cause. America of course is not perfect and has problems of her own. However, in spite of her many shortcomings, America continues to stand as a model of freedom to the world, and in this sense continues to function as God intended. On this vital issue, I believe that America continues to be on God's side.

Assuming that this is true, it is still important to remember a recurring lesson from history, mentioned often in this book. God will accomplish his purpose in his own way and in his own time. His actions in the present are never easy to discern, and few, if any, will understand them completely. God may be on America's side but, for his own reasons, may intend that America should again experience difficult times. Perhaps he is less concerned with peace and prosperity than he is with spiritual renewal.

GOD'S PERSPECTIVE

Even though God may shape nations and history, we also need to remember his perspective on human institutions. He stated it simply: "My kingdom is not of this world."[298] His ultimate concern is with the spiritual condition of individual human beings. At some point, therefore, we have to look beyond the big picture. Speculation about where America stands with God today has to ultimately focus on the issue of freedom at the personal level.

What are individual Americans doing with the freedom that so many have purchased at such great cost throughout history? We are at a time in the life of our nation when it is very appropriate for every American to seriously question the purpose of this freedom. The benefits are all around us. America has been lavishly blessed for over two hundred years and never more so than today. The question is, why?

Americans can find the answer to this question in their own spiritual roots. These roots go back to and beyond the nation's founding and are predominately Christian. Since the Revolution, the essence of freedom in America has been the freedom to seek God, personally and individually, each according to his or her own conscience. I believe that this is God's agenda and the ultimate basis of his favor for America.

God has blessed America lavishly throughout her history. As American influence has grown in the world, her example to the world has grown in importance. Economically and politically, she continues to be a light to the world. However, the question remains: What does America stand for spiritually?

Is God on America's side? Ultimately, the answer to this question lies in the hearts of individual Americans. God wants every human being to turn to him, even as he continues to give each the freedom to choose. Never before have human beings in any culture or at any time in history had such complete freedom to set their own spiritual course. It almost seems that God has perfected freedom in America. We can only speculate as to his purpose and wonder how long he will wait to see the outcome.

CHRISTIANS

Not only has God given the freedom, but he has also provided the way for each to come to him. Christians know that the clear way is through his Son, Jesus Christ. Jesus' simple message of forgiveness and reconciliation opens the way to the ultimate freedom to which human beings can aspire, a personal and intimate relationship with God, both now and in the eternal future. Christians have the duty to share this message with the world.

Beyond this simple and straightforward purpose, the role of Christians in the modern world is perhaps not so clear. Every citizen should participate in the political process and work for a better society. As citizens, Christians should form their opinions and take appropriate action on the important issues affecting their communities and the nation.

However, the lessons of our Revolution need to be remembered. Churches or groups identified as Christian are on dangerous ground when they seek power through the political process, no matter how worthy the cause. Christians only make their primary duty more difficult to accomplish if they are perceived as trying to coerce others in matters of conscience. The complex moral issues facing our culture often make this a difficult line to draw.

Christians cannot save society. However, they can be most confident they are doing God's work when they focus their attention on the human level. They attract nonbelievers to God by demonstrating the joy, purpose, and peace that permeate their own lives and churches. This process is most effective when undertaken personally and with humility. I believe that God waits to see how well his followers will accomplish this duty. He also waits to see what nonbelievers will do with the freedom and opportunity that he has given each to respond.

FREEDOM VS. FEAR

Since the Revolution, freedom has been the distinguishing characteristic of America. Countless Americans have fought to win and to preserve the liberties that have always been so important to this nation. It is dismaying now to see terrorists who are responsive to no electorate achieving their primary goal of eroding these freedoms through fear. The desire for security is powerful and continues to grow as an important issue in America today. There is continuing political pressure to sacrifice freedom for safety.

We actually see an increasing preoccupation with security in all areas of life. Americans react strongly not only to fears of terrorist attack but also to perceived threats of economic, natural, environmental, and health-related disasters. Sometimes the problems are real, but the fears are often disproportionate and irrational and are always exploited by sensation-seeking media. I believe that our preoccupation with these concerns has much to do with the anxieties and insecurities that come from a spiritual deficiency in our society.

There is a simple solution to this condition. Every American needs to realize that true security lies in something beyond military power, police protection, health care, and social security. Our founding fathers reach out over the centuries to remind us that security lies ultimately in the strength of character, purpose, and peace of mind that individual Americans can find only in God.

OTHER BOOKS FROM GOD AND COUNTRY PRESS

THE FIVE LAWS OF LIBERTY: DEFENDING A BIBLICAL VIEW OF FREEDOM

SCOTT HYLAND

ISBN-13: 978-0-89957-015-0

http://FiveLawsOfLiberty.com/

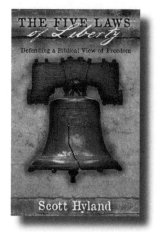

FOR MORE INFORMATION VISIT

WWW.GODANDCOUNTRYPRESS.COM

OR CALL 800-266-4977

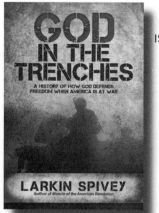

GOD IN THE TRENCHES: A HISTORY OF HOW GOD DEFENDS FREEDOM WHEN AMERICA IS AT WAR

LARKIN SPIVEY

ISBN-13: 978-0-89957-020-4

http://GodInTheTrenches.net/

BIBLIOGRAPHY

Abbot, W. W., and Dorothy Twohig, eds. *The Papers of George Washington: Presidential Series,* 2 vols. Charlottesville, VA: University Press of Virginia, 1987.

Allen, W. B., ed. *George Washington: A Collection.* Indianapolis: Liberty Classics, 1988.

Anburey, Thomas. *With Burgoyne from Quebec: An Account of the Life at Quebec and of the Famous Battle at Saratoga.* Toronto: Macmillan of Canada, 1963, first published in 1789.

Askew, Thomas A., and Peter W. Spellman. *The Churches and the American Experience.* Grand Rapids, MI: Baker Book House, 1984.

Bailyn, Bernard. *The Ideological Origins of the American Revolution.* Cambridge, MA: The Belknap Press of Harvard University Press, 1967.

Banning, Lance. *The Sacred Fire of Liberty: James Madison and the Founding of the Federal Republic.* Ithaca and London: Cornell University Press, 1995.

Barton, David. *The Bulletproof George Washington: An account of God's providential care.* Aledo, TX: Wallbuilder Press, 1990.

Barton, David. *The Myth of Separation: What is the correct relationship between Church and State?* Aledo, TX: Wallbuilder Press, 1992.

Billias, George Athan, ed. *George Washington's Generals.* Westport, CT: Greenwood Press, 1980.

Boller, Paul F., Jr. *George Washington and Religion.* Dallas: Southern Methodist University Press, 1963.

Booty, John E. *The Church in History.* New York: The Seabury Press, 1979.

Brooke, John. *King George III.* New York: McGraw-Hill Book Company, 1972.

Butterfield, L. H., ed. *Diary and Autobiography of John Adams.* Vol. I. Cambridge, MA: The Belknap Press, 1962.

Carrington, Henry B. *Battles of the American Revolution, 1775–1781.* New York, Chicago, New Orleans: A. S. Barnes & Company, 1877.

Chidsey, Donald Barr. *The Siege of Boston.* New York: Crown Publishers, Inc., 1966.

Chidsey, Donald Barr. *The Tide Turns: An Informal History of the Campaign of 1776 in the American Revolution.* New York: Crown Publishers, Inc., 1966.

Churchill, Winston S. *The Age of Revolution: A History of the English-Speaking Peoples.* New York: Dodd, Mead & Company, 1967.

Conway, Stephen. *The British Isles and the War of American Independence.* Oxford: Oxford University Press, 2000.

Cook, Don. *The Long Fuse: How England Lost the American Colonies, 1760–1785.* New York: The Atlantic Monthly Press, 1995.

Cousins, Norman. *"In God We Trust": The Religious Beliefs and Ideas of the American Founding Fathers.* New York: Harper & Brothers, 1958.

Craven, W. Frank. *John Witherspoon.* Princeton, NJ (Princeton.edu): Princeton University Press, 1978.

De Tocqueville, Alexis. *Democracy in America.* 2 vols., The Henry Reeve Text. New York: Alfred A. Knopf, 1966, first published in 1835.

Doyle, William. *The Oxford History of the French Revolution.* Oxford, NY: Oxford University Press, 1990.

Durant, Will and Ariel. *The Age of Voltaire, 1715–1756.* Part IX of *The Story of Civilization.* New York: Simon & Schuster, 1965.

Durant, Will and Ariel. *Rousseau and Revolution, 1715–1789.* Part X of *The Story of Civilization.* New York: Simon & Schuster, 1967.

Dwyer, William M. *The Day Is Ours! November 1776–January 1777: An Inside View of the Battles of Trenton and Princeton.* New York: The Viking Press, 1983.

Fast, Howard. *The Crossing.* New York: William Morrow and Company, 1971.

Fitzpatrick, John C., ed. *The Writings of George Washington from the Original Manuscript Sources, 1745–1799.* Vol. 4. Washington, DC: United States Government Printing Office, 1931.

Fleming, Thomas. *1776: Year of Illusions.* New York: W. W. Norton Company, Inc., 1975.

Flexner, James Thomas. *George Washington in the American Revolution (1775–1783).* Boston: Little, Brown and Company, 1967.

Force, Peter. *American Archives: Fourth and Fifth Series*, Washington, DC: M. St.Clair Clarke and Peter Force, 1848.

French, Allen. *The First Year of the American Revolution.* New York: Octagon Books, Inc.(reprint), 1968.

French, Allen. *The Siege of Boston.* New York: The Macmillan Company, 1911.

Frothingham, Richard. *History of the Siege of Boston, and the Battles of Lexington, Concord, and Bunker Hill.* New York: Da Capo Press(reprint), 1970.

Furneaux, Rupert. *The Battle of Saratoga.* New York: Stein and Day, 1971.

Gaustad, Edwin S. *Faith of Our Fathers: Religion and the New Nation.* San Francisco: Harper & Row, 1987.

Gaustad, Edwin S., ed. *A Documentary History of Religion in America: to the Civil War.* Grand Rapids, MI: William B. Eerdmans Publishing Company, 1993.

Gilchrist, Dr. M. M. *Patrick Ferguson.* Chadd's Ford, PA: Pennsylvania Historical and Museum Commission, Brandywine Battlefield Park, 1999.

Gordon, William. *The History of the Rise, Progress, and Establishment of the Independence of the United States of America.* 4 vols. Freeport, NY: Books for Libraries Press, 1788, reprinted in 1969.

Hampson, Norman. *The French Revolution: A Concise History.* New York: Charles Scribner's Sons, 1975.

Headley, Joel T. *Washington and His Generals.* Vol. II. New York: Charles Scribner's Sons, 1899.

Henderson, Peter. *Campaign of Chaos: 1776.* Haworth, NJ: Archives Ink, Ltd., 1975.

Hudson, Winthrop S. and John Corrigan. *Religion in America: An Historical Account of the Development of American Religious Life.* Upper Saddle River, NJ: Prentice Hall, 1999.

Irving, Washington. *George Washington: A Biography.* New York: Da Capo Press, 1976, reprinted in 1994.

Johnson, Curt. *Battles of the American Revolution.* New York: Rand McNally & Company, 1975.

Johnston, Henry P. *The Campaign of 1776 Around New York and Brooklyn.* Brooklyn: Long Island Historical Society, 1878.

Ketchum, Richard M. *Saratoga: The Turning Point of America's Revolutionary War.* New York: Holt, 1997.

Lancaster, Bruce. *From Lexington to Liberty: The Story of the American Revolution.* New York: Doubleday & Company, 1955.

Langer, William L. *An Encyclopedia of World History.* Boston: Houghton Mifflin Company, 1968.

Lefkowitz, Arthur S. *The Long Retreat: The Calamitous American Defense of New Jersey, 1776.* New Brunswick and London: Rutgers University Press, 1998.

Lossing, Benson J. *The Pictoral Field-Book of the Revolution.* 2 vols. New York: Harper & Brothers, 1860.

Lossing, Benson J., ed. *The Diary of George Washington, From 1789 to 1791.* Freeport, NY: Books for Libraries Press, 1860, reprinted in 1972.

Lunt, James. *John Burgoyne of Saratoga.* New York and London: Harcourt Brace Jovanovich, 1975.

Madaras, Larry, and James M. SoRelle, ed. *The Colonial Period to Reconstruction.* Vol. I of *Taking Sides: Clashing Views on Controversial Issues in American History.* The Dushkin Publishing Group, Inc., 1989.

McCullough, David. *John Adams.* New York: Simon & Schuster, 2001.

McManners, John. *The French Revolution and the Church.* New York: Harper & Row, 1969.

Miller, William Lee. *The First Liberty: Religion and the American Republic.* New York: Alfred A. Knopf, 1986.

Mitchell, Joseph B. and Sir Edward S. Creasy. *Twenty Decisive Battles of the World.* New York: The Macmillan Company, 1964.

Moran, Donald Norman, *Major Patrick Ferguson: The Sharp Shooter Who Almost Won the War for the British.* www.AmericanRevolution .org.

Newell, Timothy. *A Journal Kept During the Time Boston was Shut Up in 1775–6.* Vol. 1 of the Fourth Series. Boston: Massachusetts Historical Society, 1852.

Nickerson, Hoffman. *The Turning Point of the Revolution: Or Burgoyne in America.* Boston and New York: Houghton Mifflin Company, 1928.

Novak, Michael. *On Two Wings: Humble Faith and Common Sense at the American Founding.* San Francisco: Encounter Books, 2002.

Onderdonk, Henry. *Revolutionary Incidents of Suffolk and Kings Counties; with an Account of the Battle of Long Island.* Port Washington, NJ: Kennikat Press, 1849, reprinted in 1970.

Peterson, Merrill D., ed. *James Madison: A Biography in His Own Words.* New York: Newsweek, 1974.

Peterson, Merrill D., ed. *Thomas Jefferson: Writings.* New York: The Library of America, 1984.

Potter, E. B. and Chester W. Nimitz. *Seapower: A Naval History.* Englewood Cliffs, NJ: Prentice-Hall, Inc., 1960.

Pratt, Fletcher. *The Battles that Changed History.* Garden City, NY: Hanover House, 1956.

Ramsey, David, MD. *The History of the American Revolution.* 2 vols. Philadelphia: R. Aitken & Son, 1789.

Rhodehamel, John, ed. *The American Revolution: Writings from the War of Independence.* New York: The Library of America, 2001.

Rose, Matthew F. *John Witherspoon: An American Leader.* Washington, DC: The Family Research Council, 1999.

Roskolenko, Harry, ed. *Great Battles and Their Great Generals.* Chicago: Playboy Press, 1974.

Rutland, Robert A. *James Madison and the Search for Nationhood.* Washington, DC: The Library of Congress, 1981.

Schama, Simon. *Citizens: A Chronicle of the French Revolution.* New York: Alfred A. Knopf, 1989.

Schlesinger, Arthur. *The Birth of the Nation: A Portrait of the American People on the Eve of Independence.* Boston: Houghton Mifflin Company, 1968.

Schroeder, John Frederick, ed. *Maxims of Washington: Political, Social, Moral, and Religious.* Mount Vernon, VA: The Mount Vernon Ladies' Association, 1942.

Smith, Page. *Jefferson: A Revealing Biography.* New York: American Heritage Publishing Co., Inc., 1976.

Smyth, Albert Henry, ed. *The Writings of Benjamin Franklin.* Vol. I. New York: Haskell House Publishers Ltd., 1970.

Stedman, Charles. *The History of the Origin, Progress, and Termination of the American War.* 2 vols. London: Printed for the Author, 1794.

Sparks, Jared, ed. *The Writings of George Washington.* Vols. II and III. Boston: Russell, Odiorne, and Metcalf, and Hilliard, Gray, and Co., 1834.

Stember, Sol. *The Bicentennial Guide to the American Revolution.* Saturday Review Press, 1974.

Stryker, William S. *The Battles of Trenton and Princeton.* Boston and New York: Houghton, Mifflin and Company, The Riverside Press, 1898; Spartanburg, SC: The Reprint Company, 1967.

Thomas, Peter D. G. *Lord North.* New York: St. Martin's Press, 1976.

Tuchman, Barbara W. *The March of Folly: From Troy to Vietnam.* New York: Ballantine Books, 1984.

Van Doren, Carl. *Benjamin Franklin.* New York: Bramhall House, 1938.

Von Riedesel, Baroness. *Journal and Correspondence of a Tour of Duty, 1776–1783.* Chapel Hill, NC: The University of North Carolina Press, 1965.

Wallace, Willard M. *Appeal to Arms: A Military History of the American Revolution.* Chicago: Quadrangle Books, 1951.

Walpole, Horace. *Memoirs of the Reign of King George the Third.* Freeport, NY: Books for the Libraries Press, 1894, reprinted in 1970.

Ward, Christopher. *The War of the Revolution.* 2 vols. New York: The Macmillan Company, 1952.

White, R. J. *The Age of George III.* New York: Walker and Company, 1968.

Wood, W. J. *Battles of the Revolutionary War: 1775–1781.* Chapel Hill, NC: Algonquin Books, 1990.

Woods, Ralph L., ed. *The World Treasury of Religious Quotations.* New York: Hawthorn Books, Inc., 1966.

NOTES

CHAPTER ONE
CALL TO FREEDOM

1. Bailyn, p. 188, quoting Alexander Hamilton.

2. Bailyn, p. 187, quoting John Dickinson.

3. White, p. 9.

4. Louis XIV revoked the Edict of Nantes, resuming persecution of the Huguenots after about a hundred years of uneasy peace.

5. Hudson and Corrigan, pp. 62–3.

6. Ibid., p. 57.

7. Booty, p. 128; Askew and Spellman, p. 47.

8. Hudson and Corrigan, p. 90; Askew and Spellman, pp. 42–48.

9. Madaras and SoRelle, p. 86.

10. Hudson and Corrigan, p. 99.

11. The basic definition of deism.

CHAPTER TWO
FOUNDERS

12. Schlesinger, p. 245.

13. Tuchman, p. 18.

14. Miller, p. 80, quoting John Dewey.

15. Schlesinger, p. 246.

16. Ibid., p. 247.

17. Cousins, p. 80, quoting Adams's diary of February 18, 1756.

18. McCullough, pp. 101–2, quoting from *The Works of John Adams.*

19. Bailyn, pp. 289–291.

20. McCullough, p. 220.

21. Ibid., pp. 220–222.

22. Ibid., p. 225.

23. Gaustad, p. 88.

24. Cousins, p. 104, quoting Adams's letter to F. A. Van Der Kemp.

25. Novak, p. 151, quoting Adams's notes.

26. Novak, p. 150, as cited in Eidsmoe.

27. Gaustad, p. 92, quoting Adams's letter to Zabdiel Adams.

28. Smith, p. 16.

29. Ibid., p. 92.

30. Declaration of Independence.

31. Gaustad, *A Documentary History,* pp. 259–260.

32. Ibid., p. 261.

33. Jefferson's letter to John Adams, April 8, 1816, Peterson, *Writings,* p. 1382.

34. Jefferson's letter to Mrs. Samuel Smith, August 6, 1816, Peterson, *Writings,* p. 1404.

35. Jefferson's letter to Thomas Law, June 14, 1814, Peterson, *Writings,* p. 1338.

36. Jefferson's letter to Joseph Priestly, April 9, 1803, Peterson, *Writings,* p. 1121.

37. Jefferson's letter to Benjamin Waterhouse, June 26, 1822, Peterson, *Writings, p*p, 1458.

38. Smyth, *Writings,* Vol. 1, p. 232.

39. Ibid., p. 295.

40. Van Doren, p. 30.

41. Smyth, *Writings,* Vol. 1, p. 297.

42. Ibid., pp. 324–25.

43. Van Doren, pp. 110–111.

44. Gaustad, p. 61; Van Doren p. 112.

45. Van Doren, p. 529.

46. Cousins, p. 18; Van Doren, pp. 747–48.

47. Rose, p. 16.

48. Miller, p. 88.

49. Rose, pp. 25–26, quoting Witherspoon.

50. Novak, p. 133.

51. Rose, p. 68, quoting Witherspoon's sermon, "The Dominion of Providence Over the Passions of Men," delivered on May 17, 1776, on the eve on independence.

52. Craven, p. 2.

53. Peterson, p. 23, letter to William Bradford, Nov. 9, 1772.

54. Peterson, p. 25, letter to William Bradford, Sept. 25, 1773.

55. Peterson, p. 29, letter to William Bradford, Jan. 24, 1774.

56. Cousins, p. 301, from the Journal of the Virginia Convention, 1776. The approved article ended with the statement that, "it is the mutual duty of all to practice Christian forbearance, love and charity towards each other."

57. Peterson, p. 41.

58. Cousins, p. 311, quoting "Memorial and Remonstrance."

59. Peterson, pp. 94–95.

60. Ibid., p. 136.

61. Cousins, p. 321, letter to Frederick Beasley, Nov. 20, 1825.

CHAPTER THREE
LOSERS

62. Tuchman, p. 128, quoting Edmund Burke.

63. Ibid., p. 131.

64. Walpole, p. 3.

65. Brooke, p. 43.

66. Ibid., p. 62.

67. Ibid., p. 90.

68. Ibid., p. 101.

69. Brooke, p. 135, quoting Lord Holland.

70. White, p. 81; Brooke, p. 102.

71. Brooke, p. 125.

72. Tuchman, p. 158.

73. Cook, pp. 113–14.

74. Brooke, p. 138.

75. Tuchman, pp. 173–74.

76. Ibid., p. 174.

77. Brooke, p. 123.

78. Tuchman, p. 181.

79. Ibid., pp. 167, 174.

80. White, p. 120.

81. Tuchman, p. 185.

82. White, p. 138.

83. Cook, p. 149.

84. Repeal was voted on March 5, 1770, by strange coincidence the same day as a famous incident on the other side of the Atlantic: the Boston Massacre.

85. Thomas, pp. 69–70.

86. Thomas, p. 115; Tuchman, p. 184.

87. Cook, p. 237.

88. Tuchman, p. 210.

89. Cook, p. 238.

90. Conway, p.146.

91. Conway, p. 59, 2.5 million pounds was about one quarter of total exports.

92. Tuchman, pp.158, 181.

93. Conway, p. 333, The idea of virtual representation was first formally proposed by Thomas Whately, Grenville's secretary of the treasury in a 1765 pamphlet.

94. White, p. 25.

CHAPTER FOUR
FOUNDING FATHER

95. Sparks, Vol. II, p. 89, letter to John Washington, July 18, 1755.

96. Irving, p. 119.

97. Sparks, Vol. II, p. 353.

98. Lancaster, p. 38.

99. Sparks, Vol. II, p. 398, letter to Bryan Fairfax, Aug. 24, 1774.

100. Irving, p. 150.

101. Ibid., p. 166.

102. Lancaster, p. 129.

103. Sparks, Vol. III, p. 5–6.

104. Sparks, Vol. III, p. 3, letter to Martha Washington, June 18, 1775.

105. Schroeder, pp. 309–10, General Orders, July 4, 1775.

106. Sparks, Vol. III, pp. 24–25, report to the president of Congress, July 10, 1775.

107. French, *First Year*, p. 523.

108. Sparks, Vol. 3, pp. 221–22, letter to the president of Congress, Jan. 4, 1776.

109. Fitzpatrick, Vol. 4, p. 243, letter to Joseph Reed, Jan. 14, 1776.

110. Sparks, Vol. 3, p. 152, letter to Colonel William Woodford, Nov. 10, 1775.

111. Sparks, Vol. 3, p. 153, letter to Woodford.

112. Gilchrist, p. 1.

113. Moran, p. 4, quoting the report of Captain Ferguson. Ferguson was the commander of a company of sharpshooters, armed with a new rifle designed by Ferguson himself in England. Ferguson was later killed at the battle of Kings Mountain.

114. Allen, pp. 196–98, General Orders, Oct. 20, 1871.

115. Irving, p. 596.

116. Gaustad, *Faith*, p. 44.

117. Irving, p. 610.

118. University of Virginia, *Documents*, Farewell Orders to the armies, Nov. 2, 1783.

119. Irving, p. 619.

120. Rhodehamel, *Writings*, p. 794.

121. Allen, p. 239–249, Circular to the States, June 14, 1783.

122. Gaustad, *Faith*, p. 55.

123. Irving, p. 642.

124. Allen, p. 333, Letter to John Jay, Aug. 15, 1786.

125. Allen, p. 382, Letter to the Marquis de Lafayette, Feb. 7, 1788.

126. Irving, p. 646.

127. Abbot, *Papers*, pp. 173–77. First inaugural address (final version), Apr. 30, 1789.

128. Gaustad, *Faith*, p. 103.

129. Cousins, p. 69.

130. Fitzpatrick, *Writings*, Vol. 5, pp. 245, General Orders, July 9, 1776.

131. Fitzpatrick, *Writings*, Vol. 26, p. 239–249, Circular to the States, June 14, 1783.

132. Allen, pp. 131–33.

133. Gaustad, *Faith,* p. 76.

134. Abbot, *Papers*, Vol. 2, p. 424, Letter to the United Baptist Churches of Virginia, May 1789.

135. Gaustad, *Documentary History*, p. 277, letter to the Religious Society called Quakers, Sept. 28, 1789.

136. Gaustad, *Documentary History*, p. 278, letter to a Committee of Roman Catholics, Mar. 15, 1790.

137. Gaustad, *Documentary History*, p. 279, letter to Moses Seixas, Aug. 17, 1790.

138. Cousins, p. 78.

139. Durant, p. 784.

CHAPTER FIVE
BUNKER HILL

140. Cousins, p. 62, quoting 1790 letter to Hebrew congregations.

141. Gordon, p. 46.

142. Frothingham, p. 137.

143. Chidsey, *The Siege of Boston*, p. 95.

144. Frothingham, p. 139.

145. Ibid., pp. 192–94.

146. French, *First Year*, p. 256.

CHAPTER SIX
BOSTON

147. Irving, p. 175.

148. Ibid., p. 180.

149. Ramsey, p. 207.

150. French, *First Year*, p. 260.

151. Ibid., p. 655.

152. Chidsey, *Siege of Boston*, p. 143.

153. Frothingham, p. 290.

154. Gordon, p. 193.

155. French, *First Year*, p. 656.

156. Fitzpatrick, *Writings*, p. 350.

157. Frothingham, p. 297.

158. French, *First Year*, p. 659; Gordon, p. 192.

159. Gordon, p. 193.

160. Ibid., p. 193.

161. French, *First Year*, p. 660.

162. Gordon, p. 193.

163. Newell, p. 272.

164. Gordon, p. 196.

165. French, *First Year*, p. 672.

166. Irving, p. 245.

167. McCullough, p. 130.

168. Samuel Adams, Speech in Philadelphia, 1776.

169. Gordon, p. 202.

170. French, *First Year*, p. 659.

CHAPTER SEVEN
LONG ISLAND

171. Johnston, p. 125.

172. Gordon, pp. 240–241; Johnston, pp. 132–38.

173. Johnston, pp. 95–96, General Orders, July 2, 1776.

174. Ward, p. 211; Johnston, p. 140.

175. Johnston, p. 154; Ward, p. 215.

176. Johnston, p. 155.

177. Gordon, p. 277.

178. Ward, p. 223.

179. Johnston, p. 203; Ward, p. 22; Gordon, p. 311.

180. Chidsey, *The Tide Turns*, p. 41.

181. Ibid., pp. 32–33.

182. Ibid., p. 22.

183. Ward, p. 232; Johnston, p. 209–210.

184. Johnston, p. 214; Chidsey, p. 43.

185. Johnston, p. 214, see also Force's Archives.

186. Johnston, p. 222.

187. Gordon, Vol. II, p. 314; Johnston, p. 222.

188. Gordon, Vol. II, p. 314–315; Johnston, p. 222.

189. Onderdonk, 131; Lossing, *Pictorial Field Book*, Vol. II, p. 607; incident also cited by other early histories citing no source.

190. Johnston, p. 223, citing the entire personal account of Major Benjamin Tallmadge of the Connecticut Brigade and other contemporaneous diary entries of first person observers.

191. Gordon, pp. 315–316.

192. Johnston, p. 224.

193. Ibid., p. 200.

194. Ward, p. 236.

195. Tuchman, pp. 210–211.

196. Ibid., pp. 209–210.

197. Ibid., pp. 212–213.

CHAPTER EIGHT
TRENTON AND PRINCETON

198. Irving, p. 324.

199. Thomas Paine, "The American Crisis."

200. Lancaster, p. 240.

201. Stryker, pp. 94, 99.

202. Ibid., p. 106.

203. Ibid., p. 107.

204. Ibid,, p. 110.

205. Ibid., pp. 110–111.

206. Fleming, p. 459; Dwyer, p. 220.

207. Johnson, p. 53.

208. Stryker, p. 120.

209. Chidsey, *The Tide Turns*, p. 118; Wood, p. 66; Johnson, p. 54; Dwyer, p. 263 cites this story as a legend.

210. Wallace, p. 131; Irving, p. 328.

211. Irving, p. 332.

212. Dwyer, p. 253.

213. Lancaster, p. 246.

214. Stember, p. 30.

215. Wallace, p. 132; Ward, p. 311. Several claimed credit for this suggestion in later years. Col. Joseph Reed was especially familiar with the area. He had lived in Trenton at one time and attended Princeton.

216. Gordon, p. 400.

217. Wallace, p. 133.

218. Ward, p. 316.

219. Lancaster,p. 254.

220. William Pitt, Speech in Parliament, quoted by Tuchman, *The First Salute*, p.151.

221. Churchill, p. 191.

222. Durant, Will and Ariel, Part X, p. 922.

223. Fleming, p. 427.

224. Fleming, p. 458; Henderson, p. 969.

225. Irving, p. 333.

226. Wood, p. 65; Fast, p. 123; Dwyer, p. 221.

CHAPTER NINE
SARATOGA

227. Von Riedesel, pp. 47, 55.

228. Furneaux, p. 23.

229. Ketchum, pp. 81, 84; Furneaux, p. 25.

230. Furneaux, p. 26.

231. Lossing, Vol. I, p. 37.

232. Lunt, p. 124.

233. Furneaux, p. 51.

234. Ketchum, p. 136.

235. Furneaux, p. 88. St. Clair was charged with neglect of duty and acquitted, but did not completely salvage his reputation.

236. Furneaux, p. 90.

237. Ketchum, p. 267.

238. Nickerson, pp. 470–72. Several versions of Jane McCrea's death have been told. Nickerson presents the evidence and decides in favor of the version offered. Regardless, the results were the same.

239. Lossing, Vol. I, p. 48.

240. Stedman, p. 327. Burgoyne later gave his rationale for the decision. He thought it would be perceived as a retreat to move back up Lake George to Ticonderoga before continuing his advance southward.

241. Ketchum, pp. 282–83.

242. Lossing, Vol. I, p. 41.

243. Ketchum, p. 335.

244. Stark's brigade was designated an "independent command" to ensure that it would not be absorbed into the Continental units defending along the Hudson.

245. Ketchum, p. 315.

246. Lossing, Vol. I, p. 48.

247. Nickerson, pp. 436–37; Furneaux, pp. 152–160; Ketchum, p. 346. American numbers were in flux during this campaign and are difficult to ascertain at specific dates. I have used the more conservative estimates that most sources agree upon.

248. Furneaux, p. 149.

249. This battle has been called the first battle of Saratoga and the battle of Stillwater. Freeman's farm is used most commonly.

250. So far, Burgoyne had advanced down the east bank of the Hudson River. However, several areas lay ahead on the eastern side of the river considered impassable to troops. The west bank was thought to be the only viable route south.

251. Nickerson, p. 437.

252. Ketchum, p. 347. Named for a local tavern keeper, Jotham Bemis.

253. Anburey, p. 180.

254. Ibid., p. 176.

255. Ketchum, p. 375.

256. Nickerson, p. 437.

257. Stedman, p. 340.

258. On October 3 Clinton did launch an expedition up the Hudson and successfully captured Fort Montgomery and Fort Clinton by October 7. This operation did not relieve Burgoyne directly, but did prove helpful in eventual surrender negotiations.

259. Historians disagree on the effectiveness of Arnold's actions on October 7. I believe that the evidence shows that the battle would have been largely inconclusive without this penetration of the British lines.

260. Stedman, p. 344.

261. Nickerson, p. 405.

262. For example, see Mitchell, and Creasy, Pratt, and Roskolenko.

263. Anburey, p. 175.

264. Proverbs 16:18.

CHAPTER TEN
YORKTOWN

265. Lancaster, p. 447, quoting Thacher's *Military Journal of the American Revolution.*

266. Ward, p. 696.

267. Wallace, p. 210. This capitulation of U.S. forces was only exceeded by the surrenders of General Julius White at Harpers Ferry in 1862 and General Jonathan Wainright at Corregidor in 1942.

268. Ward, p. 866, quoting letter to John Cadwalader.

269. Cook, p. 332.

270. Ibid., p. 335.

271. Potter and Nimitz, p. 89.

272. Cook, p. 343.

273. Ward, p. 883.

274. Ibid., p. 883.

275. Wallace, p. 256.

276. Cook, p. 347, quoting the personal diary of Major Patrick Mackenzie.

277. Lancaster, p. 448, quoting Colonel Elias Dayton.

278. Wallace, p. 261.

279. Peterson, p. 61, Vol. 1.

280. Peterson, p. 53, Vol. 1.

281. Potter and Nimitz, p. 90.

CHAPTER ELEVEN
ANOTHER PERSPECTIVE

282. Churchill, p. 267.

283. Potter and Nimitz, p. 35–186.

284. Potter and Nimitz, p. 107; Churchill, pp. 267–273.

285. Churchill, p. 273.

286. Ibid., p. 268.

287. McManners, pp. 24–31, 38–39; Doyle, pp. 143–147.

288. McManners, p.85.

289. Schama, "Terror is the Order of the Day;" McManners, pp. 100–101; Hampson, pp. 139–140; Langer, p. 632.

CHAPTER TWELVE
MIRACLES OF THE REVOLUTION

290. De Tocquevile, Vol. I, pp. 44, 305.

291. De Tocqueville, Vol. I, p. 320.

292. De Tocqueville, Vol. I, p. 303.

293. In Exodus, chapters 7–14, God demonstrated his power to Pharaoh through a series of plagues. Yet each time he caused Pharaoh's heart to be hardened (twelve times). This is usually attributed to God's plan to demonstrate his power and his favor of the Israelites. God said, "The Egyptians will know that I am the Lord." I speculate that nation building was also an important part of God's agenda.

294. Samuel Adams, Speech in Philadelphia, 1776.

295. Novak, p. 150.

CHAPTER THIRTEEN
A NEW CALL TO FREEDOM

296. This is the most famous passage attributed to De Tocqueville and quoted by Presidents Eisenhower, Reagan, and Clinton. Its origin, however, is uncertain.

297. The subject of this book and *God in the Trenches: A History of How God Defends Freedom When America Is at War.*

298. Spoken by Jesus, John 18:36.

INDEX

Note: entries followed by *m* indicate a map

ABOUT THE AUTHOR

 Larkin Spivey is a decorated veteran of the Vietnam War, a retired Marine Corps officer, and former military professor at The Citadel. He was trained in special forces, ranger, and airborne operations, was with the blockade force during the Cuban Missile Crisis, and served in the White House. He now lives in South Carolina, actively writing and speaking about God's hand in American history.